Higher Education
on the Brink

Praise for *Higher Education on the Brink*

"Dr. Alicia B. Harvey-Smith is a seasoned leader with a rare talent; she knows how to navigate through the potholes of institutional pastures, and she also has a gift for capturing her journey in writing. In this book she anchors her vision for change in her astute observation that 'In essence, everything that we do, and how we do it, must be reconsidered.' This is not just a book about re-engineering enrollment management. This is a book about how to achieve institution-wide student and institutional success with changes in policy, programs, practice, and personnel. For those colleges and those leaders who have suffered from this pandemic, this book is an antidote that provides a prescription for recovery."—Terry U. O'Banion, PhD, Senior Professor of Practice, Kansas State University; President Emeritus, League for Innovation in the Community College

"Today's college leaders must be prepared to address an increasing number of challenges to the viability of their institutions. One of the most consequential is enrollment planning in the face of a projected drop in college-age students and fluctuations in enrollment caused by economic cycles or unexpected crises such as a pandemic. In this publication, Dr. Alicia B. Harvey-Smith provides needed practical advice for leaders to address this existential threat and to strengthen their institutions."—George Boggs, PhD, Superintendent/President, Palomar College; President and CEO Emeritus, American Association of Community Colleges; Chair, Phi Theta Kappa Board of Directors

"Dr. Harvey-Smith provides a clarion call noting that the long-known rules of the game have changed and community-college-as-usual will lead to sub-optimum outcomes or worse. She suggests a practical and collaborative approach to business model redesign, a reduction in student-customer suffering, tactical uses of online instructional and related technologies, targeted and enriched student outcomes, and an improved and inclusive student demographic mix through a restructured strategic enrollment methodology."—Daniel J. Phelan, MBA, PhD, President & CEO, Jackson College

"The pandemic has, in some ways, forced all post-secondary institutions to quickly and creatively re-imagine how they will attract, retain, and graduate current and future students. This book prepares those institutions who strive to be innovative and entrepreneurial a road map on how to re-imagine strategic enrollment management and remain competitive and sustainable. In this ever-changing landscape of teaching and life-long learning, Dr. Alicia Harvey-Smith's book, *Higher Education on the Brink: Reimagining Strategic Enrollment Management in Colleges and Universities,* will help guide internal discussions and establish priorities that will maximize student engagement and financial sustainability."—John J. "Ski" Sygielski, EdD, President, Harrisburg Area Community College (HACC), Central Pennsylvania's Community College

"The steep increase in the number of adults who might question the very value of a college degree, along with the steady uptick in the American entrepreneurial spirit, is forcing higher education to invest more in career assessment, life and career coaching, and career pathways. This is a necessary morphing of enrollment management. Simultaneously, societal cries for diversity, equity, and inclusion, with an ironic assist from COVID-19, further exposed disparities faced by low-income students, in part resulting from the digital divide and other access barriers. *Higher Education on the Brink: Reimagining Strategic Enrollment Management in Colleges and Universities,* tackles the hard questions and provides best-in-class solutions for critics and innovators alike. Will colleges survive the pandemic? Yes! Will the students return? Yes! But only if we get it right."—Brian Johnson, EdD, President, Advance Higher Ed., LLC

"Historically, college and university leaders have worked hard to meet the needs of students and the communities in which they reside. In these settings, leaders take pride in sharing how their faculty provide a personal touch in the classroom, given the small class sizes that afford special attention to individual students. On the other hand, these leaders face difficult challenges with increased student needs, achievement gaps, and retention of first-generation students. To provide increased support for students, colleges and universities have ramped up evidence-based reforms. In order to make sustainable change in higher education, the culture warrants inclusion of multiple voices in the development of the strategic priorities and goals, which has historically been time consuming, yet valuable. Fast forward to March of 2020 and, in a blink of an eye, given a global pandemic, our culture had to change, and change quickly. We needed to ramp up and continue to draw upon our capacity to utilize data and evidence to make some of the most difficult decisions of our careers in order to protect the safety, health, and well-being of students, faculty, and staff. *Higher Education on the Brink: Reimagining Strategic Enrollment Management in Colleges and Universities,* by Alicia B. Harvey-Smith, PhD, provides a lens into the impact of the pandemic and how leaders must embrace positive and lasting change in higher education. This book offers an opportunity to reflect and consider the evidence-based strategies that will be required to support student enrollment, retention, persistence, and success. Finally, the author provides the space for leaders to consider the culture of higher education and how to engage both internal and external stakeholders, in new ways, to support necessary change and institutional sustainability—both critical factors for a successful future."—Annette Parker, EdD, President/CEO, South Central Community College

"With no playbook to guide us, planning and responding to COVID-19 and post-COVID-19 challenges at hand are serious, complex issues that affect us all. A book that offers new innovations and ideas to re-imaging strategic enrollment management is a resource that many institutions of higher learning would appreciate. This book offers strategic steps and strategies to address complex issues colleges face and provides guidance to develop new enrollment management plans to attract and retain students."—Quintin Bullock, DDS, President, Community College of Allegheny County

"Emergent enrollment declines, the pandemic, and resulting disruptions are challenging leaders. This down-to-earth, practical book suggests a variety of ways to meet Strategic Enrollment Management and other challenges, where ideas rely on shared responsibility, "significant cultural changes," strategic approaches, and what the author describes as a "village approach." Acknowledging the need to diversify revenue streams, Alicia B. Harvey-Smith also reflects a strong component of caring as colleges seek ways to assure access for those from the lowest-income groups and success for all who enroll."—Roberta C. Teahen, PhD, Director and Faculty, Doctorate in Community College Leadership Program, Ferris State University

"'Don't let a crisis pass without recognizing possibilities' is something I stressed when I taught crisis management to my public relations students. COVID-19 is a once-in-a-century crisis. The tragedy and heartache of this pandemic for many will never go away. But through the difficulties, COVID-19 forced a new way of thinking—and new paradigms emerged. Dr. Harvey-Smith introduces just that in a field of higher education accustomed to moving at a glacial pace. And with the current state of higher education, her work is very much needed."—Nicholas C. Neupauer, EdD, President, Butler County Community College

"In *Higher Education on the Brink: Reimagining Strategic Enrollment Management in Colleges and Universities,* Harvey-Smith shows why great leadership is the key to organizational success. Known as one of the nation's foremost authorities on change in higher education, Harvey-Smith provides solutions to current and future threats facing colleges and universities with a comprehensive examination of the many challenges that are fundamentally altering the nation's higher education landscape. In the process, she presents a strategic framework for leaders to follow to ensure their institutions have adequate resources and provide quality outcomes for students. This book should be required reading for anyone concerned about addressing the challenges facing higher education during these times of unprecedented uncertainty."—Vince Mumford, EdD, Director, Sports Management Division, Central Michigan University; founder, The Good Prize

"The devastation of the coronavirus pandemic has necessitated innovative changes to the work required to best serve our students and strengthen our institutions. It is crucial to remember the broader socio-economic issues highlighted by the crisis as we seek to reinvent higher education. This book's thought-provoking strategies and wisdom about approaching a post-pandemic academic world makes it a must-read for leaders in higher education."—Shirley Robinson Pippins, EdD, Senior Consultant, Academic Search

Higher Education on the Brink

Reimagining Strategic Enrollment Management in Colleges and Universities

Alicia B. Harvey-Smith, PhD

ROWMAN & LITTLEFIELD
Lanham • Boulder • New York • London

Published by Rowman & Littlefield
An imprint of The Rowman & Littlefield Publishing Group, Inc.
4501 Forbes Boulevard, Suite 200, Lanham, Maryland 20706
www.rowman.com

86-90 Paul Street, London EC2A 4NE, United Kingdom

British Library Cataloguing in Publication Information Available

Library of Congress Cataloging-in-Publication Data

Name: Harvey-Smith, Alicia B., 1962–, author.
Title: Higher education on the brink : reimagining strategic enrollment
  management in colleges and universities / Alicia B. Harvey-Smith.
Description: Lanham : Rowman & Littlefield, [2022] | Includes bibliographical
  references and index. | Summary: "Higher Education on the Brink provides
  advice on how to structure strategic planning initiatives, including
  alternative revenue streams, to serve the modern learner. When colleges
  plan strategically and think differently, they better serve students, support
  the institution's sustainability, and create an environment in which teams
  will thrive"—Provided by publisher.
Identifiers: LCCN 2021032796 (print) | LCCN 2021032797 (ebook) |
  ISBN 9781475856620 (cloth) | ISBN 9781475856637 (paperback) |
  ISBN 9781475856644 (epub)
Subjects: LCSH: College attendance. | Universities and colleges—Admissions.
  | Universities and colleges—Planning. | Strategic planning.
Classification: LCC LC148 .H37 2022 (print) | LCC LC148 (ebook) |
  DDC 378.1/61—dc23
LC record available at https://lccn.loc.gov/2021032796
LC ebook record available at https://lccn.loc.gov/2021032797

♾™ The paper used in this publication meets the minimum requirements of
American National Standard for Information Sciences—Permanence of Paper
for Printed Library Materials, ANSI/NISO Z39.48-1992.

To the colleges and universities which are committed to creating authentic learning environments, where a student's success is as important as their enrollment. And to all students who dare to dream their dreams to completion, and once completed, dare to dream again.

"It's only on the brink that people find the will to change. Only at the precipice do we evolve."—John Cleese, actor

"New beginnings are often disguised as painful endings."—Lao Tzu, Chinese Philosopher

Contents

Foreword

The higher education industry is at an inflection point. Once upon a time, the academy could truly operate as an Ivory Tower, accessible only to some and difficult for everyone else to scale. Postsecondary education was restricted to the elite, and the structures and systems surrounding the institution were designed to maintain that restriction.

Times have changed. We recognize the value of access to education, both from a socioeconomic development perspective and from an economic growth perspective. Higher education is truly a public good. But many of the structures around the industry—designed for times past—remain in place.

Institutional rankings are still (at least partially) based on exclusivity. That is, how many applicants an institution rejects directly plays into its ranking as a "high-quality" postsecondary institution. Financial aid is still built around credit-bearing programing, despite the demand for (and value of) nondegree education in supporting learner outcomes.

However, we're starting to see change in our industry and that change is being driven largely by the work happening at colleges and universities specifically focused on their communities. Technical colleges, community colleges, and continuing/workforce education divisions are on the forefront of higher education's evolution.

These institutions find creative ways to extend access to postsecondary programming for traditionally underserved audiences. They work to make education more affordable, rather than using tuition and fees as a "quality check" for prospects. They design courses, programs, and

...tials to have clear labor market outcomes, to help students imme-
...y recognize and realize a return on their educational investment.

Higher education is becoming more personalized, with a focus on ensuring students get what they need from the institution just in time. The next step to that is in defining and delivering clear pathways—pathways that allow them to continue to access education as and when they need it, and pathways through their careers.

That is why it's so important for every college and university leader to familiarize themselves with the insights shared in *Higher Education on the Brink: Reimagining Strategic Enrollment Management in Colleges and Universities.* Enrollment management practices common at higher education institutions nationwide were designed for the old higher education ecosystem—the outdated, traditional, place-based one that kept folks on the outside looking in.

Truly, a modern higher education institution cannot rely on the traditional "lead-funnel" model of enrollment management, designed around semesters and reliant on events like college fairs. The modern higher education enrollment funnel must be digitally enhanced, with a high-quality website designed to attract prospective learners and help them find relevant offerings quickly and easily. This also means programming models must evolve to be less reliant on the traditional semester schedule and, instead, be offered flexibly and launched quickly.

Alicia Harvey-Smith is a renowned education leader, and through this book she is truly leading the charge in helping higher education leaders think differently about how their institutions operate and who their institutions serve. Rather than loading readers down with theory, you will receive practical, common-sense advice on how to structure strategic planning initiatives—and the various practices that drip from it—to serve the modern learner.

And let's not get this confused, we are truly in the business of serving modern learners. Today's higher education institutions serve a diverse audience of students. There are always those individuals seeking out traditional, degree-based experiences. But there are others looking for just-in-time learning experiences. There are more still who want to find short-term opportunities to earn credentials and grow and then stack those into longer-term learning experiences as their careers evolve.

What's more—as you'll learn from this book—serving these audiences and onboarding the technologies that support them will not only support a richer array of revenue streams to support sustainability but also create an environment your teams will thrive in. And from that, you'll create an environment that doesn't just serve students for a two- or four-year period, but one that serves students for a lifetime.

We're fortunate to have a rich postsecondary ecosystem, with options for ongoing learning available to all. It's incumbent upon us all, though, to recognize the work that's happening at community-oriented institutions. And to not only support that work, but to try to emulate their philosophies and missions in creating access to high-quality, affordable, outcome-oriented programming for all. In this book, Harvey-Smith provides us with a playbook to help execute this vision at every institution in the country.

That is what you, the reader, will take away from this. And our industry—and society—will be better for it!

Amrit Ahluwalia
The EvoLLLution

Preface

Strategic enrollment management (SEM) is a significant framework in the organization and practice of higher education. As resources become less and less available, colleges and universities must find innovative ways to achieve enrollment and revenue requirements.

Coupling strategic enrollment management with other revenue-generation strategies will enable institutions of higher education to remain open and viable in an ever more competitive space.

Moving forward, it will be essential that colleges develop strategies to provide the financial support needed to accommodate the projected diversity and growth of student bodies, where the cost of education is becoming out of reach for many families.

The role of technology and emerging software innovation is also igniting strategic enrollment management's recognition as both science and art, as the alignment of practices of strategic planning and strategic enrollment management are achieved.

Although complex, it is essential to expand innovative enrollment management strategies to allow the greater maximization of resources within a framework that supports diversifying revenue generation.

I propose a shift in planning and practice that focuses not only on optimum enrollment, that is, admitting students, but also on securing the success of a diverse student body by detailing strategies that enable their success and employment.

Reimagined strategic enrollment management practices must focus not simply on the traditional enrollment funnel and the leads collected, but on the actual matriculation and completion of students. This will encompass the intentional reduction or elimination of barriers that prevent student and organizational success.

Additionally, there is a need for institutions to align within their strategic planning practices the priority of establishing alternative streams of revenue beyond enrollment to enhance financial sustainability and provide additional financial balance.

The impetus for this book arose from reflection on enrollment and projection trends that warn of an even greater challenge for colleges and universities to stay afloat. This was particularly pronounced where enrollment was the dominant or sole driver of institutional revenue.

This challenge is further complicated for institutions that do not have the availability of endowments, grants, state funding, or other such financial support, thus making it more difficult to sustain the quality and continuity of programs and services when enrollment benchmarks are not met.

John Cleese stated that "It's only on the brink that people find the will to change. Only at the precipice do we evolve." I believe this statement might not simply apply to people but to colleges and universities as well. COVID-19 moved higher education to the brink and forced a level of change previously unseen.

This level of change is ushering in a new beginning for postsecondary education. For many colleges, it will require a transformed and more evolved model for both strategic planning and strategic enrollment management practice.

COVID-19 brought with it unprecedented change and challenge, impacting enrollment decisions and institutional sustainability. Many students and families are continuing to delay college admissions, opting instead to take a gap year or more. This has caused massive disruption to higher education and is requiring colleges and universities to rethink every element of the college experience.

In essence, everything that we do, and how we do it, must be reconsidered. Today, as in the past, colleges have been confronted with wartime pressure, civil unrest, demographic shifts, economic downturns, weather disasters, and the like. During these periods, college operations were reduced, merged, and temporarily or permanently discontinued. COVID-19 forced many of the same responses throughout the higher education landscape. It forced immediate and significant change.

Historically, there have been repeated calls for change in higher education; however, radical and transformational change for the majority of institutions was slow to occur. Now, economic, political, demographic, and technological forces are prompting swifter responses and unique transformations.

As a result of COVID-19, our institutions were immediately forced to reexamine our enrollment, instructional, and financial systems. The next steps of this radical adjustment will be guided by an innovative model of strategic visioning and planning as our institutions grapple with ongoing financial burdens and organizational sustainability.

The shift required by COVID-19 necessitated an unheard of level of social, emotional, and academic adjustment. In the blink of an eye, colleges were providing massive online education and student services with varying degrees of success.

This book encourages a thorough institutional reexamination of the total student experience to optimize student success and to develop new frameworks that enhance financial sustainability and stewardship.

This call to action supports systemic changes in engaging new ways of planning, leading, and modeling institutions to thrive in the times ahead, as colleges and universities address declining outcomes of enrollment and net revenue.

To this end, the Center for Enrollment Research, Policy and Practice, among other entities, has focused new efforts on restoring public trust in admissions and higher education to address the complex issues surrounding the need for systemic change.

Higher Education on the Brink: Reimagining Strategic Enrollment Management in Colleges and Universities provides ideas for colleges and universities to consider as they begin the important work of institutional reflection and reexamination in light of the COVID-19 pandemic.

This book presents an original change model, to assist colleges and universities in achieving institutional priorities by reducing resistance to change. It also makes a clear case for redefining enrollment management through innovatively implementing revenue-diversification strategies and outlines inclusive approaches for ramping up strategic planning engagement to increase buy-in, ownership, and the likelihood of long-term success.

Higher Education on the Brink concludes with a case history and details strategies for repositioning institutions.

This book calls for a comprehensive shift in thinking and planning coupled with a strategy for the development of alternative streams of revenue. It supports the application of approaches that address the new and emerging challenges of enrollment management, strategic planning, and achievement of institutional priorities through uniquely defined strategic directions.

From a systemic approach, replicable results can be brought to scale. As a result, colleges and universities can develop a responsive model to address the discrepancies in accessibility that are the result of family income.

As documented by AACU in its *Facts & Figures* newsletter, the larger percentage of prospective college students coming from low-income backgrounds where English may not be the primary language, are often being placed at the bottom quartile (28 percent) of students admitted to college. In contrast, 78 percent of students from the top income quartile were enrolled in college in 2016.

The numbers of students within the lowest quartile are projected to increase as the number of students with the ability to pay the full price of education decreases. This speaks to the dire need for a reimagined approach to higher education, strategic enrollment management, and leadership.

In order to thrive, higher education institutions and systems must be open and responsive to change and learning. As demographers and labor market experts agree, the projected enrollment declines will continue. The educational pipeline must be expanded in new ways and additional revenue streams must be identified.

As enrollment benchmarks become harder to reach, it is imperative that institutions seize the opportunity for strategic innovation and add the goal of developing multiple streams of revenue in all strategic planning and enrollment management efforts to sustain operational continuity. The stakes are rising for institutions of higher education as we envision a vibrant new beginning within a new normal.

There are many available books and articles explaining in relative detail the importance and significance of strategic enrollment management or strategic planning. There are also a growing number of references that suggest the concept of revenue diversification for colleges and universities, sharing examples of how some institutions are moving in this direction.

There are fewer examples of colleges and universities comprehensively restructuring strategic planning efforts to embrace an inclusive college-driven model that uniquely combines these critical strategies.

This book will not stall in the jargon of strategic enrollment management or strategic planning. We have many wonderful books conveyed in this manner to reference. However, the goal with this book is to convey in clear and direct language a story of one president's attempt to make meaning of higher education's current state and bringing these vital concepts together to share in a practical way how significant outcomes can be achieved.

This book is not full of charts and data, but it is full of strategies for pulling teams together, communicating clearly and repeatedly, incorporating inclusive strategies to increase buy-in and ownership, listening, focusing on the changing higher education landscape, taking data-informed risks, and pushing for greater innovation.

This book is written for the practitioner, the college president and teams who will benefit from its clear language and examples that encourage a higher level of CARE (compassion, appreciation, respect, and empowerment) as essential leadership standards, in order to create and nurture organizational cultures that are open and responsive to change and learning.

This is a reference to the Seventh Learning College Principle, which directs attention to establishing an organizational culture that is supportive of the diffusion of innovation and strategic excellence.

I have often reflected on why some institutions experience greater success in planning and accountability. I have determined that it is their intentional concern for organizational cultures that are collaborative in nature.

What I have learned is that intentionally creating environments where people have a voice and are encouraged to engage and provide feedback matters. Authentically engaging the whole college community matters, breaking down artificial barriers and silos matters, crafting a plan, its goals and objectives together matters, and most importantly, an organization that learns together and grows together matters.

At no other time in the history of higher education—as we face an uncertain future—do these things matter more. It is well known that not all strategic planning involves SEM, but all SEM must involve strategic planning.

This book hopes to demonstrate why consciously interweaving these concepts makes good sense, as does incorporating innovative revenue-generation strategies.

My hope is that you find its contents helpful and a reminder of the need to repeatedly reflect upon our work and adapt as circumstances change. This must be done while maintaining a focus on the organization's true bottom line, represented by the people within our institutions, who tirelessly create teaching and learning environments that comprehensively support operational and student excellence.

Acknowledgments

I am honored to acknowledge the President's Cabinet and Board of Trustees of Pittsburgh Technical College for embracing a collective and transformative vision as we plan a future by our design; the courageous leaders of our strategic planning taskforce and the more than seventy volunteers who dared to dream with me; colleagues from across the country who lead by example, thank you for endorsing this important work; Lynn McMahon, thank you for helping to nurture this project to completion; and to my amazing husband and muse, Donald, for his continuous patience and love.

Chapter 1

Introduction

*Strategy is not a lengthy action plan. It is the evolution of a
central idea through continually changing circumstances.*

—Jack Welch, former chairman and CEO, General Electric

Transforming higher education and its enrollment and planning has
never been more important. Colleges and universities have no other
choice but to reinvent themselves. COVID-19 has forced a reckoning by placing many colleges and universities on the brink of a new
beginning.

The survival of many higher education institutions will necessitate a
severe reimagining of all approaches. A new model for strategic planning and sustainability must emerge and will require a coming together
of many previously disconnected entities within the higher education
infrastructure.

Higher education leaders must take a fresh look at how their institutions design, implement, and measure practices in strategic enrollment
management and expand the model, as never before.

Strategic enrollment management is best approached through an
integration of strategies and interdisciplinary practices throughout the
course of strategic planning. By thoroughly reexamining the college's
planning infrastructure, processes, and culture, and by engaging stakeholders, a new and more effective model may emerge.

1

Such innovative models and new thinking will assuredly improve the development and management of the strategic planning process, which should also be redesigned to consider ideas for revenue enhancement beyond traditional enrollment.

Further, these models should be guided by a set of strategic directions that enable the systemic development of a more relevant planning structure that can efficiently support the outcomes of attracting, recruiting, enrolling, retaining, and graduating diverse students.

An effectively designed enrollment management model requires far more than a focus on enrollment or matriculation; it requires a laser-like focus on successful completion, and it touches every facet of the organization and its financial sustainability. The development of comprehensive strategies is the first step; however, equally as important are the next steps of implementation and evaluation of strategies and outcomes.

Achieving a radical and comprehensive redesign of strategic planning, enrollment management, and its practices and outcomes will require the engagement of the whole organization and its systems and institutional stakeholders from every segment of the college to assess, examine, explore, and design.

Bringing this perspective to life for colleges and universities struggling to understand and respond during these unprecedented times is critical. It will lead to a new standard of plans that addresses strategic and enrollment planning that looks beyond the current enrollment conundrum and includes innovative strategies for revenue generation. This is a powerful approach to planning, particularly for more vulnerable institutions.

Effective plans that yield measurable outcomes in each of these areas are the most compelling rationale for this book. Developing innovative plans requires a commitment to dismantle old models and to think differently about the role colleges can and must play in the lives of its community. It also requires a willingness to partner in creative ways with internal and external constituents.

This book seeks to uniquely combine strategies for enrollment enhancement with significant support for the development of alternative revenue streams for overall sustainability and growth. It also introduces a new model for launching a highly engaged strategic planning process for colleges and universities.

Beyond the analytics, market research, and targeted recruitment strategies that must be leveraged to achieve important outcomes, this book seeks to direct colleges to define high-impact approaches in enrollment and innovative revenue generation. It urges colleges and universities to be guided by an integrated strategic planning process that simultaneously engages the college community at heightened levels in order to recalibrate efforts to yield key results. The major difference in this work is an exacting focus on the culture and each facet that defines it.

According to Education Unlimited, of the 5,300 colleges and universities in the United States, 1,627 are public, 1,687 are private, and 985 are for profit. The various models used by most colleges and universities to sustain their operations and to guide overall financial practices are traditional in nature and primarily enrollment driven.

To survive the current tumultuous environment, colleges must implement strategies to expand revenue generation beyond the dollars generated by the number of tuition-paying students entering each quarter, semester, or year, and strategically identify alternative streams of revenue to enhance financial sustainability.

Colleagues leading public institutions have the added benefit of some level of state appropriations to further buoy their operations, beyond the enrollment or tuition revenue received. However, resources remain a challenge as colleges and universities seek to operate at optimum levels.

As we examine the massive disruption in higher education caused by COVID-19, the drastic downturn in the economy, the long-standing and documented concerns expressed by parents and students alike, there remains a clarion call for colleges and universities to do better, in terms of costs and outcomes.

This can be achieved by the radical overhaul of strategic planning efforts, developing more innovative and entrepreneurial financial models, and redesigning its current infrastructure and replacing it with one that is more aligned with current and projected realities. Colleges and universities of all types will not escape the impact of the new normal, the reality of higher education post-COVID-19.

A CHANGING LANDSCAPE

Higher education as we have known it has now and forever dramatically changed and so must the previous models that we once held dear.

COVID-19 is disrupting higher education unlike anything ever experienced. However, the resulting challenges also provide an opportunity for higher education to reimagine, reinvent, and create a new model that best responds to the evolving needs of its stakeholders.

Institutions that have been historically slow to change were compelled to shift from a static infrastructure to accommodate virtual instruction and to address the challenges represented by enrollment, finances, and student support, all at once.

Even before the COVID-19 pandemic, American higher education was facing significant challenges, with fewer students attending colleges in 2019 when compared to 2010 and public support for higher education decreasing in large part due to concerns with high tuition levels.

Although colleges derive revenue from tuition and fees, they also rely greatly on third parties, taxpayers, and private donors to support their missions. Minus this support, many institutions may be forced to close.

COVID-19 has further weakened financially vulnerable colleges, particularly those that are serving at-risk populations. Operating in a post-COVID-19 environment has forced these colleges to face a new set of unanticipated expenses, and they must plan for the future during an even more uncertain period. The increased likelihood of a closure or merger makes it even more dire for colleges and universities to reexamine the traditional enrollment model.

Other recent outcomes have included many high school seniors reconsidering their first-choice schools in favor of colleges that are less expensive and closer to home. It also is highly probable that many students will also reexamine the types of schools and majors selected, opting to select more applied and career-focused institutions in response to the new economy and emerging workforce demands. Research also has indicated that students are reducing study to part-time or taking time off to work and assist family members impacted by unemployment and illness, as a result of the pandemic.

Many low-income students will have an even greater challenge with returning to college during and post-COVID-19, as well as rising seniors who are having increased difficulty taking the necessary steps to complete admissions processes. These decisions will have lasting repercussions throughout higher education and within the U.S. economy, as noncompleters are relegated to lower-wage jobs.

A FAMILIAR NEMESIS

The challenges of enrollment in higher education will no doubt worsen as a result of COVID-19; however, this challenge has persisted for years, predating the current pandemic. Over the last decade, student enrollment has been trending downward. A recent study conducted by Inside Higher Education and Gallup revealed that only 34 percent of the institutions polled met their enrollment targets for the Fall 2017 term by May 1 (declining from 37 percent in 2016 and 42 percent in 2015). Additionally, 85 percent of senior admissions staff reported that they are very concerned about reaching institutional enrollment targets.

Another survey of 400 chief business officers conducted by Inside Higher Ed in 2017 revealed that 71 percent of the institutions surveyed believed that higher education institutions are facing significant financial difficulties. This represents an increase of 8 percent from 2016.

The Western Interstate Commission for Higher Education confirmed that in 2017, there were 80,000 fewer high school graduates than in the previous year. This represented a decline of more than 2 percent. Wisconsin, Illinois, and Indiana were the states experiencing the most significant drops.

Another significant challenge faced by many publicly funded higher education institutions is the continuous decrease in state funding. Multiple years of decreased state funding for public institutions and community colleges have resulted in reduced critical student support and wrap-around services. This places an added burden on institutional resources to achieve student success and completion goals.

Decreased state funding for flagship universities was pointed to as a partial reason for the United States' drop in world rankings. Times Higher Education's publication of the fourteenth annual World University Rankings of 1,000 institutions from 77 countries revealed a decrease in America's domination of the rankings. For the first time in the history of the report, no U.S. school ranked in the top two spots.

Another challenge visible across all segments of higher education is the decline in international student enrollments. For the Fall 2017 term, 40 percent of U.S. colleges and university deans cited declines in international student enrollments. This is consistent with estimates cited by ICEF Monitor that the United States' share of the international student market declined from 28 percent in 2001 to 22 percent in 2018.

FOCUSING ON A NEW FUTURE

In light of the continuous and significant enrollment challenges being faced across all of higher education, the reimagining of enrollment, planning and revenue-generation models and approaches is paramount as institutions fight for survival.

As colleges look to improve revenue generation and plan for the future, a focus on virtual learning and supports for students is essential. Inside Higher Ed's study of chief academic officers revealed 82 percent of them planned to grow online course offerings to expand access to adult and nontraditional students in the next year. This study was conducted prior to the COVID-19 pandemic.

Below are some examples of challenges identified in the survey, as well as opportunities that colleges and universities might seize.

• Skills Gap: 64 percent of surveyed employers believed that an organizational skills gap exists. This is an opportunity for universities to work with businesses to develop courses and programs that prepare workers for highly valued roles. It is also an opportunity to expand internships and apprentice training that might also convert to full-time career positions.
• Competency-Based Education: Competency-based education has long been inconsistent across the higher education landscape. This low-hanging fruit is an opportunity for colleges and universities to collaborate with business and industry partners to clearly define standards and measurements when awarding credit for work experience.
• Program Design: It is important that program offerings continue to evolve and align with industry demands in order to engage continued learning. Colleges and universities can expose students to the idea and value of life-long learning by taking a learner-centric approach to education. This level of engagement can inspire and ignite passion for learning. This is also an opportunity for business and industry advisory boards to help guide curriculum design toward greater relevancy with industries and aligning workforce demand.

As colleges and universities place new focus on strategically reimagining higher education and their role in it, it is also important to radically examine the need for strategic partnerships. Strategic business partnerships are also a unique opportunity for colleges to collaborate with business and industry where missions align.

As suggested by Insperity, a provider of human resource solutions, these strategic relationships create joint value and the potential to increase growth and efficiencies.

Insperity suggests strategic business partnerships can do the following:

- Build Organizational and Leadership Confidence: All business leaders encounter fears related to change and uncertainty, whether those changes are due to a pandemic or are market-driven, regulatory, or industry-specific. Integrating strategic solutions through strategic business partnerships can minimize the impact of changes that can inhibit your business and institutional growth.
- Expand Expertise: During this period in higher education, colleges can benefit from developing high-value content through a joint value proposition aimed at a unique target market. Partnering with large associations, agencies, or industry experts is a good way to shorten your go-to-market life cycle for new program offerings and possibly improve outcomes. In a partnership for this purpose, one organization outsources its noncore competencies with the expectation that the partner organization will deliver a product, service, or peer-group expertise that will demonstrate value for both the businesses and the college.
- Leverage Resources: Leveraging another organization's capabilities or resources can enable you to achieve the desired goal without taking on the full expense or overhead. Colleges and universities are brokers of education, although targeted to different audiences. For example, technical colleges, community colleges, public, and private institutions all have specific missions, yet at the core of each is education.

A partnership might involve a community college partnering with a senior institution to design a comprehensive dual or joint admissions pathway. The student completes the first two years at the community college and seamlessly transitions to the senior institution to complete the remaining two years. The model is jointly developed, branded, and marketed. The costs are shared by the partners and marketed to a broader audience.

- Create Predictable Revenue Streams: Predictable revenue is a framework for creating consistency, year-over-year and providing business growth based on a formulaic process. Additional revenue streams are needed more than ever, as colleges are challenged with enrollment declines. A strategic business partnership is designed to be lucrative for the organizations and partners involved. The more organizations or associations that you selectively partner with, the broader exposure, expanded target market and the greater potential to increase revenue.
- Establish Subject Matter Experts and Thought Leadership: Many college faculty, staff, and administrators are subject matter experts and thought leaders. By collaborating with business partners, new co-created content, solutions, and new ways of thinking emerge.
- Co-Market Plan: A co-marketing plan between partners may involve e-mail, direct mail, social media, and more—targeting all partner market audiences. Through a well-crafted agreement, partnership institutions can expand to new markets, establish new enrollment pipelines, and heighten the visibility of institutions.

Through this partnership structure, college presidents and other organizational leaders can also engage in a nonthreatening, noncompetitive environment to authentically collaborate, share challenges, and creatively find solutions for growing and making operational improvements.

Chapter 2

The State of Higher Education

*Ensuring quality higher education is one of the most important
things we can do for future generations.*

—Ron Lewis, American politician

A significant level of disruption was delivered to higher education in
2020 as colleges and universities rapidly transitioned to virtual operations. In early March 2020, the University of Washington was one of
the first major universities to suspend in-person classes. After which, a
cascade of more than 1,100 colleges and universities in all fifty states
rapidly modified their educational approaches.

With uncertainty as to the scope or duration of the effects of COVID-
19, colleges and universities were faced with the decision of how to
maintain continuity in educational operations. Immediately, colleges
explored what form reopening would take. These plans ranged from
socially distanced, in-person instruction to hybrid models that limited
on-campus participation to online-only instruction.

While on the surface these solutions appeared to merely be logistical,
upon further examination it was clear that the rapid onset of COVID-19
exposed many critical gaps in our colleges and universities that lingered
below the surface.

Many of these gaps were not new but had been lingering unaddressed. Computer labs, shared resources, and on-campus facilities
could bridge critical socioeconomic issues, like the digital divide. But

when these "bridges" were no longer accessible, it exposed key failures, unveiling critical socioeconomic issues, left unaddressed.

A quarter of our nation is still without broadband Internet, according to a recent study by the Pew Research Center. Even as Internet providers worked to develop options to address this gap, many students still faced barriers to education, including equipment, environment, and engagement.

Students with socioeconomic challenges were faced with trying to do schoolwork on a cell phone, finding public Wi-Fi to provide reliable Internet connections and not being able to complete assignments due to a lack of proper computer equipment in the home.

These challenges were compounded by ad hoc instructional and infrastructural solutions that were quickly developed by colleges and universities. Even the most senior faculty and staff were challenged with adapting in-person curricula, instructional methods, and services for delivery online.

Addressing labs and applied and technical participation was just the beginning. When combined with the additional challenges of modifying campus layout, reducing density and other needed responses to COVID-19, the return to onsite instruction will also initially represent additional disruption.

AN INDUSTRY UNDER SIEGE

The challenges created by COVID-19 were set against a backdrop of the passing of the Golden Age for colleges and universities. Costs continue to increase, while the ability and willingness to pay for them is decreasing. Many institutions are unable to produce sufficient productivity gains to cover this emerging gap.

Although rising costs and funding challenges have existed in higher education, institutions are now, more than ever, being challenged with technology demands, disruptive competition, increasing needs associated with evolving demographics, heightened service and support expectations, rising student debt, default rates, and, most significantly, continuing doubts about higher education's return on investment.

Colleges and universities are at a crossroads. The destiny of our institutions will be tied to an ability to radically transform and optimize every facet of the operation.

As we prepare for the future in this disruptive space, we must foster innovation in order to survive in the new normal. We must cultivate organizational cultures that embrace the unknown and boldly reshape the next chapter.

In light of continued declines in anticipated state funding, demand for improved performance outcomes and projections that fewer traditional-age college students (eighteen to twenty-two years old) will enter college beginning in 2025 due to lower birth rates, the future will require college and university leadership to envision the possibilities and plan accordingly.

As we continue to study and understand the impact of COVID-19 on the decision to enroll, 57 percent of high school students in the Pew survey expressed concern that the pandemic will impact their future plans for college attendance.

A summary of the Pew Research Center survey data revealed that as many as 44 percent of high school juniors and seniors said the pandemic has impacted their college affordability plans with more than 58 percent of teenagers being more likely to take out student loans for school.

Almost three-quarters of teenagers said they have had discussions with their parents or guardians about the financial impact of the virus. Additionally, 24 percent said their parents or caregivers had shared their concerns about whether or not they would be able to pay the bills, and 13 percent had a parent or guardian lose their job.

The current state of higher education has unearthed new stressors for families. In addition to stress about their parents' jobs, teenagers are also worried about their own jobs. The survey found that 22 percent of teenagers hold a job, and 46 percent said their families depend on their income to help manage household expenses. For working teenagers, 62 percent said they have to violate their state's social distancing protocols and recommendations in order to continue at their place of employment.

In addition to financial concerns, high school students are also stressed about the overall health of family members. According to the survey, 59 percent of teenagers said they worry about a parent or guardian getting sick, while 60 percent are worried about other family members eventually contracting the virus.

There are numerous factors influencing traditional-aged college students, but another data point worth examining is the widening enrollment gap caused by the projected withdrawal of adult learners aged twenty-five and older. These learners have typically enrolled at greater rates during weaker economic periods when there is higher unemployment.

The converging of all of these factors presents a critical challenge for colleges and universities. This is a challenge that will require an examination of institutional practices and the generation of innovative solutions. One such solution is the reimagining and expansion of strategic enrollment management and strategic planning approaches to guide outcomes.

EXPANDING SUPPORT FOR STUDENTS

To better help students cope with the stressors of this period, colleges might consider expanding counseling services to support students, their families and college faculty and staff. Student support is an important component of the educational process. During remote instruction, place greater emphasis on checking the well-being of students and making sure students are adjusting in an effective manner. To support this, you may need to add members to the education and support teams to conduct additional student outreach.

Colleges also may choose to expand the online educational infrastructure to focus on providing quality academic experiences that achieve critical learning objectives and help students continue their progression toward completion.

Make every attempt to provide students access to all materials needed in the online learning environment. This has included, for some institutions, sending textbooks and course materials home to students, as well as providing additional equipment and supplies, including technical equipment such as cables, hotspots, and Chromebooks to better support learning and assist students experiencing technical challenges.

STRATEGIES FOR STAYING CONNECTED AND SUPPORTING STUDENTS NEW TO ONLINE INSTRUCTION

During this unprecedented time in higher education, colleges, and universities are encouraged to develop new systems for communicating and responding to students and families. The following are strategies you might consider to support the adjustment of students new to online instruction and maintaining a connection to the college community.

- Provide frequent communications to the college community, as well as housing communications and other information on a dedicated page on your website.
- Hold town hall meetings with students, parents, faculty, and staff to assure they have accurate information and are given an opportunity to provide feedback.
- Design all online sessions to simulate and, where possible, improve upon the on-ground classroom experience. Prior to class start, give students all online course content and instructions for engagement, including discussion boards, lecture notes, activity sheets, project packets, and digital course resources.
- Share accountability for student and operational success. Engage the entire college in supporting the learning and adjustment of students.
- As students are enrolled, design a clear strategy for long-term retention and success. Each department and member of the college community makes a difference to student satisfaction and their progression toward completion.

TACTICS FOR FACULTY TO
SUPPORT ONLINE LEARNING

Here are some specific examples of how faculty can lead during COVID-19 to ensure students remain connected and engaged with learning:

- In order to ensure that course delivery is conducive for the online environment, academic departments should review programs and make strategic adjustments. Many programs may be able to fully transition to the new format with minor or no course realignment.
- Information systems technology faculty, at one institution, facilitated remote student learning, using the same software used in the classroom to perform lab assignments at home.
- The Electronics Department at the same technical college created new electronic labs to be completed at home with minimal teacher

guidance to provide significant mastery of hands-on competencies. They also sent lab materials, such as digital trainers, parts, test equipment, and power supplies, to students to set up at home labs.
- Interdepartmental and cross-disciplinary collaborations are important to creating a culture of support. For example, at Pittsburgh Technical College, the Electronics and IT Departments partnered to implement PLC simulator software—the most frequently used automation technology in manufacturing—to simulate the on-ground experience. Similar partnerships may prove beneficial across institutions.
- Video production faculty at another institution met students near their homes to drop off equipment to further enable a quality at-home and virtual-learning experience.
- Academic departments should consider providing binder versions of eBooks to students, who may require a hard copy of textbooks for improved learning. Faculty might consider incorporating publisher demonstrations of chapter exercises directly into course content and demonstrating exercises on a white board.
- Institutions may consider using both synchronous and asynchronous modalities to provide additional flexibility when needed and to better support learning. As virtual instruction continues, colleges may wish to record all sessions to provide students access to materials, whenever needed.

ENHANCING THE VIRTUAL STUDENT EXPERIENCE

Although there is nothing quite like the on-campus college experience, there are steps you can take to try to replicate that experience in a virtual environment.

- Create virtual study halls to allow ease of connectivity and opportunity for faculty and peers to check on students periodically or upon request.
- Replicate skills labs and tutoring sessions in the virtual structure and provide students with support from faculty and peer tutors.
- Introduce a virtual student union and clubs for students to come together to connect and celebrate.
- Hold virtual open houses and community events to introduce your campus, sponsor virtual town halls to share updates, and celebrate

special occasions, like commencement, online to recognize your graduates.

During this unique time in higher education, the entire student experience will need to be redesigned. Explore additional enhancements specific to your culture and traditions. Challenge conventional thinking. Extraordinary circumstances require extraordinary creativity.

REDEFINING OUR FUTURE

Our industry must examine how we transform our approaches during this current state. This will entail a comprehensive review of institutional strategy and the exploration of vision, mission, and core values as we define our future state.

How quickly and how successfully our industry is able to reach that future state will depend upon several factors. The most important are leadership, student responsiveness, engagement of stakeholders, boldness to deconstruct the current state, identification of barriers, and building for future success.

Role of Strategic Enrollment Management in a Re-envisioned Future

What role does strategic enrollment management (SEM) play in our efforts to reach that future state?

SEM assists in changing higher education's view of the admissions process and supports an integrated approach to cultivating and sustaining students throughout enrollment.

In order for colleges and universities to achieve financial sustainability, leaders must evaluate external and projected future influences, create an enrollment strategy that articulates institutional priorities and allocate specific resources to strategies in order to achieve enrollment goals.

SEM is a tool to create and sustain student enrollment. The functions that compose the ecosystem of SEM involve generating a demand for courses and programs and aligning the recruitment function to create sustainable enrollment.

This leads to demand generation, which is the creation of inquiries, applications, and visits to campus. This function is critical to building capacity and sustainable enrollment. The application and admissions process allows colleges and universities to systematically gather information leading to the formal entry of students into college.

THE ROLE OF INSTITUTIONAL FINANCES

Financial aid and net revenue are critical components of SEM. The strategic use of unfunded and funded financial assistance as a method of generating revenue, sustaining enrollment, and creating access is an important utilization of financial aid. This occurs in a myriad of ways including focusing on both merit and need.

The most essential elements of this type of planning are effective information management, measurement, and tracking of outcomes. A comprehensive student information system will allow student progression to be tracked from the "input—throughput—output" of the student's lifecycle and allow the development of reports that enable open and responsive follow-up.

COMPREHENSIVE, COLLABORATIVE MARKETING

Also important is the implementation of highly effective marketing and communications strategies. Colleges must build and sustain interest and demand through awareness and brand identity and should be driven by effective Strategic Enrollment Management strategies.

This component of SEM requires vision and collaboration across divisions, with shared responsibilities and clearly defined roles in marketing communications, academics, student services, and advancement areas, minimally.

CONTINUALLY RECRUITING TO RETAIN

We often say that it is easier to keep a student than recruit a new one, and just as recruitment is everyone's business, so is retention. It is the most important part of recruiting.

Retention is, in essence, the systematic analysis and support of students once enrolled. It is the intentional removal of barriers to their success. SEM, therefore, requires a plan to provide students with the support needed to remain enrolled until graduation.

This collaborative effort expands across the entire institution. Each department should be engaged to support and assess the quality of the student experience.

SEM requires a research and analysis function to systematically track student behavior, performance, satisfaction, and improve decision-making. A comprehensive student tracking system can support early alert, mid-semester performance tracking and other systems and indicators to improve attrition. The information is critical and allows colleges and universities to respond quickly to improve outcomes.

Chapter 3

The Case for Reimagining Strategic Enrollment Management

> *We need to contribute to a different future by fundamentally re-imagining education. That means putting the learner at the center of everything we do.*
>
> —Jay Bhatt, technology executive

Strategic enrollment management (SEM) is largely credited with starting at Boston College in the 1970s. At its most basic, SEM is looking beyond the current state of your institution to prepare for the changes in the surrounding environment. It is now a primary driver in the field of higher education.

National, regional, state, and local trends present a variety of outcomes that may radically disrupt enrollment and retention. While no amount of planning could prepare for the level of disruption caused by COVID-19, the more that colleges and universities understand critical external factors influencing the decisions of students and their families, the more effective colleges will become at surviving major disruptions in the future.

THE NEED FOR STRATEGIC ENROLLMENT MANAGEMENT

The most effective SEM model will provide an institution with a blueprint to guide the optimization of resources to better retain a diverse body of students, while also maximizing the benefits of enrollment. A well-structured SEM model will use data-driven goals to support critical success factors including services, quality, competitiveness, and retention strategy.

As institutions work harder to attract students, balance curricula with the needs of the market and focus on long-term student success in a very challenging economy, the science and art of SEM will only become more necessary.

The complexity of mission has inspired many schools to focus on more effective strategic enrollment management plans. These plans will better serve students, more clearly identify goals, more accurately measure success, and maximize institutional resources.

CONSIDERATIONS WHEN DEVELOPING SEM PLANS

For colleges that are developing initial strategic enrollment management plans or reevaluating current SEM plans, the following are strategies to consider:

Use the Student as Your Compass

Focus on students and let them guide efforts based on their needs. The most effective SEM plans will use both market research and student feedback to guide the decision-making process.

Offer programs of the greatest interest to students at varying times in different modalities that are also aligned with industry demand.

Examine your infrastructure to determine capacity and conduct a service and policy audit to determine if any landmines exist that are barriers to student success.

Identify the procedures or challenges within your culture that are hindering your achievement of outcomes. Explore what changes can be made to facilitate the whole student experience.

Integrate Data into All Your Decisions

Be guided by data, both quantitative and qualitative and the derived outcomes. Place assumptions, intuition, opinions, and hunches on the shelf. Always use solid data and clear outcomes. Develop a disciplined data-driven approach to decision-making as a framework for all plans.

Study enrollment, demographic, and occupational trends to provide a snapshot of enrolled students. This data will show not only who you are serving and how well but also who you are not serving. It is equally as important to understand the regional market and target the emerging demands of the workforce to anticipate and develop innovative and competitive programs. Use of competitive analyses can identify competitors, discover areas of opportunity for jobs of the future, and respond to market changes.

Review inquiry statistics, student enrollment and attrition rates to understand what is working, what is not and why. Successful strategic enrollment management is a moving target, and data is essential as you refine strategies and goals.

Commit to Excellence and Accountability

No college or university can be perfect on every metric, but all colleges and universities can achieve improved outcomes by promoting a culture of excellence and accountability and aligning resources to improve assessment. It takes a village to achieve a higher standard.

Enrollment, like retention, is the responsibility of the total college community. Your ability to establish and maintain a successful strategic enrollment management plan will require the elimination of silos and the involvement of each department.

As part of your implementation strategy, you should incorporate clear objectives, identify responsible parties, and measure progress toward goals and key performance indicators (KPIs). Strategic Enrollment Management and Strategic Plans should be living documents, and therefore, reviewed and adjusted on a regular basis. These plans should be standing items at staff meetings, cabinet meetings, and board meetings. There should be continual reflection and discussion to keep plans alive in your institution.

Use Technology for Efficiency Gains

An integrated student information system (SIS) can improve operational efficiency and the student experience. The gains in communication and time will pay off with greater efficiency and enhance the engagement and support of the student learning experience.

Consider the utilization of inquiry generation tools, CRM solutions, case management tools, and social media platforms to encourage and improve the communication flow and seamless exchange of information.

Leverage existing technology and access to new technology to remove repetitive steps for students, faculty, and staff as well as to troubleshoot issues. This also will reduce the resource expenditures of staff. For example, how might sharing information between the registrar's office and financial planners better support students? How might a comprehensive student advising and support model collaboratively designed and implemented by both academic affairs and student affairs units better improve student success outcomes?

Create a Culture That Is Open and Responsive to Change and Learning

Emotional intelligence is critical to effective leadership. Institutional leaders should be engaged and trained with these skills. High levels of self-awareness, self-management, and self-performance, coupled with compassion, appreciation, respect, and empowerment should be viewed as essential leadership standards. The foundation of any successful organization is its people.

Establish a transparent and inclusive strategic planning process and encourage members of the college community to lead key components of the process. This will increase ownership and investment in the outcomes. Consider inviting the entire college to engage in some element of plan development. Making the plan a standing item at all college meetings will allow opportunities to share and receive feedback. This approach enables the plan to emerge as a shared vision brought to life by your college community.

The process further allows for the community to ask opinions, seek input, and shape a plan for a future envisioned together. More importantly, once the plan is implemented, because of the early engagement during its development, the community will feel a greater sense of ownership, remain involved through periodic updates, and successes can be celebrated together.

The team-building benefits of this high level of intentional engagement in institutional planning will carry over into other initiatives and may have broad, positive impact throughout your college or university.

Strategic enrollment management is a process that involves your entire institution, and the long-term success of the plan will be enhanced through this collective effort. As your institution explores ways to increase enrollment, boost student satisfaction and success, and achieve its mission, vision, and values, let a well-considered and data-driven SEM plan guide the way.

Sew SEM into the Fabric of Your Culture

The management of enrollment works best when it is comprehensive and fully integrated into the fabric of the college with a laser focus on students and their success. These intricate plans provide clear and certain direction by containing goals that support the implementation of strategies, processes, and systems that directly improve the recruitment, retention, persistence, and completion of students in all programs, be they credit, noncredit, workforce development, or specialized contractual training programs. These plans also set parameters you and your team can use to measure progress and success.

In response to increasing competition, student diversity and the desire to improve retention, persistence, completion, and student success, it is imperative that colleges direct attention to shaping the student experience and the utilization of comprehensive strategic enrollment management plans that are designed to support the college strategic plan.

This student experience must be intentionally shaped in ways that yield improved outcomes in converting applicants to registrants, reducing the numbers of students stopping out from one term to the next, and creating processes and procedures that support payment and the redesign of programs and services in order to be more responsive to the needs of students.

Your strategic enrollment plan, as a living document brought to life by the work of the collective, must be reasonably flexible to respond to changes in environmental factors, such as funding, demographic shifts, external influences, or unanticipated fluctuations.

This inclusive and comprehensive planning process should be developed to enable the achievement of optimum results in outreach, recruitment, retention, and graduation.

As institutions face intensifying enrollment and retention challenges, there will be continued calls for significant cultural changes that foster more learner-centered approaches and shared responsibility for enrollment outcomes.

The active involvement of faculty in SEM planning is imperative. In many traditional strategic enrollment management processes, faculty and academic departments were often absent. The success of this work falls largely on the full engagement of the college community.

It is also vitally important that institutional leaders are both visible and active at all levels of the planning process. Their ability to articulate and champion this work will make a significant difference to its ultimate success.

An Ongoing Commitment to Students

High-performing enrollment organizations commit to the cultivation of student relationships throughout the student lifecycle and the engagement of the college community. The need for this level of engagement in SEM planning, decision-making, and change has never been greater.

Ongoing relationships will anchor the process and serve to improve all aspects of the student experience, both in and out of the classroom.

A clearly articulated marketing plan will raise awareness and fuel the cultivation of relationships throughout the recruitment process. As brand loyalty and commitment are established, greater engagement, enhanced retention, and more effective alumni relationships will be fostered.

ENROLLMENT CHALLENGE

Nationally, higher education institutions of all types are facing increasing challenges with reaching enrollment benchmarks. According to Inside Higher Education (June 21, 2018), community college enrollments specifically will continue declining over the next several years

This challenge is further complicated by declines in state funding and rising demands for improved performance outcomes. Further compounding the situation are projections that a lower number of traditional-age college students (eighteen to twenty-two years old) will be entering college beginning in 2025 due to lower birth rates during the recession.

The withdrawal of adult learners aged twenty-five and older who have typically enrolled at greater rates during weaker economic periods with high unemployment will also contribute to widening the gap in enrollments.

The conversion of all of these factors presents a critical challenge for colleges and universities. This is a challenge that will require an examination of institutional practices and the generation of innovative solutions.

One such solution is the reimagining and expansion of strategic enrollment management approaches to provide an answer, or at the very least, lead institutions in the right direction.

STRATEGIC ENROLLMENT MANAGEMENT SOLUTION

Placing renewed focus on comprehensive strategic enrollment management (C-SEM), as I have come to define it, can assist colleges with addressing ongoing enrollment challenges with clear goals targeted on the enrollment, retention, and completion of students.

The term "C-SEM" represents an approach that is intentional, comprehensive, and integrated, requiring an examination of all institutional systems, processes, policies, and procedures to determine if they are effective in addressing SEM goals or if unintentional barriers exist and need to be adjusted.

A large number of students start college and do not finish, once enrolled. This represents another important element to the enrollment challenge.

Research conducted by the consulting firm EAB found that out of one hundred students who apply to a community college, fifty-six are lost during onboarding, twenty-three dropout and only five are still enrolled after six years, in some form of education or employment. Furthermore, only nine of the one hundred complete an associate degree and seven complete a bachelor's degree.

C-SEM strategies will improve outcomes in this area by helping institutions to conceptualize the onboarding process from the first contact with students, application completion, placement tests, financial aid and billing processes, completion of orientation, registration, retention, and persistence measures, through graduation and to the ultimate cultivation of alumni.

Strategic Approach

The C-SEM approach should engage the total college community strategically in comprehensively addressing issues of enrollment, barriers to growth and continuous matriculation and potential challenges with institutional processes and systems that impede retention and completion.

Figure 3.1 details the four core objectives in C-SEM Planning. The standards integrate a focus on capacity building through enrollment and growth, a thorough examination of processes and systems to evaluate efficiency in supporting institutional outcomes and implementation and

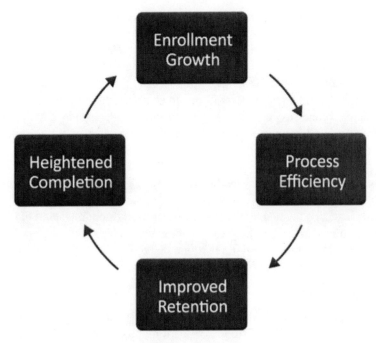

Figure 3.1   C-STEM Core Objectives.

evaluation of retention strategies to increase graduation and completion rates.

C-SEM Core Standards

The utilization of an Annual Cycle of Effectiveness process, designed to support strategic planning, can support the assessment of outcomes for C-SEM.

It is important to view C-SEM as a collegewide imperative and operationalized within environments that foster learner-centered approaches, where there is a shared responsibility for enrollment outcomes.

Institutions will need to commit to an in-depth organizational examination and to sound strategic enrollment management practices and standards that build community by inspiring, engaging, leading, and planning, as shown in figure 3.2.

Effective strategic enrollment management planning should inspire a collegewide focus on the full student experience. A high-performing enrollment organization cultivates student relationships from the initial point of contact throughout the student life cycle.

The active and ongoing engagement of faculty in SEM planning is essential. As institutions reimagine these processes, they should actively engage the academic community in SEM planning, decision-making, and strategic change.

It is important to note that a common focus on student learning helps to anchor the enrollment management effort to improve all aspects of the student experience, inside and outside the classroom.

The most important aspect of effective strategic enrollment management planning and execution is leadership. Institutional leaders must lead the charge. Visible support, engagement, and collaboration of institutional leaders at all levels are critical in the SEM process.

Laying the foundation for an extensive planning process is important. Colleges must determine leadership capacity to enact change, foster a culture of collaboration, and establish the conditions needed to manage

Figure 3.2   Community Building Standards.

change. The figure below shows the process and conditions needed for change (Harvey-Smith, 2016).

C-SEM Infrastructure

Comprehensive strategic enrollment management planning should be an integrated process, embracing a collegewide perspective in order to develop and manage a systemic set of activities designed to intentionally attract, recruit, enroll, retain, and graduate students, and ultimately, engage them as alumni. It requires a laser-like focus on student matriculation and successful completion.

ONE COLLEGE'S APPROACH: LONE STAR COLLEGE

Before moving through an extensive planning process, Lone Star College (LSC) in Houston laid the foundation for its success by first determining their leadership capacity for making the change needed and then making efforts to foster a culture of collaboration to manage change.

Lone Star established a strategic long-term view of recruitment, admissions, retention, and completion and developed a continuum to track students from the inquiry stage through cultivation, enrollment and retention, culminating with completion, graduation, and alumni giving.

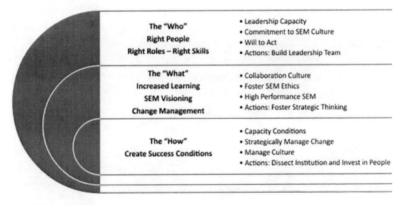

Figure 3.3   Process and Conditions for Change.

As the executive vice chancellor of academic and student affairs, I established and led the Strategic Enrollment Management Council and launched its efforts in February 2017 to explore enrollment patterns, practices, and processes across six campuses, eight satellite centers and two university centers.

A diverse and talented team of faculty, staff, and administrators from campuses, centers, and system office comprised LSC's Strategic Enrollment Management Council, allowing for broad input and feedback.

Supporting the work of the council were campus-based SEM teams, whose primary task was to develop localized plans supporting the overall system goals and seven designated SEM subcommittees with collegewide and interdisciplinary participation focused on examining and developing innovative strategies.

Figure 3.4 lists the SEM subcommittees established to support the charge. These subcommittees examined the internal processes affecting their area of focus to make formal strategic recommendations.

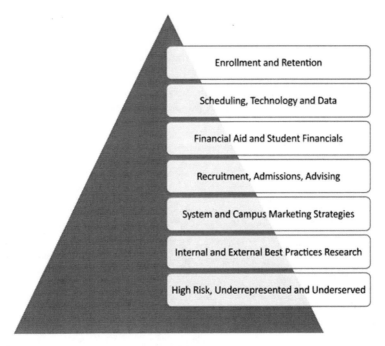

Figure 3.4   Lone Star SEM Subcommittees.

The Charge

The charge of the SEM Council was to develop a comprehensive and integrated strategic enrollment management model. The model included the recommendation of goals and strategies for collegewide processes, systems, and assessment measures supporting recruitment, retention, persistence, and completion in credit, noncredit, workforce development, and training programs.

The process in figure 3.5 enabled the development of a solid SEM infrastructure and recommended measures for assessing its progress.

Process Overview

LSC's strategic enrollment management process was divided into stages of activity progressing from assessing the current state, identifying and planning the future state, executing an action plan to reach the future state, assessing the future state for goal attainment, and finally, to a continued process for quality improvement and assessing the "Vision—Planning—Action—Future State" cycle.

Figure 3.6 provides a sample of high-impact, long-term strategies used in the plan. The unit objective in this figure provides an example of an early warning system for low grades to provide an intervention measure.

Assessment plays a critical role in implementing a successful C-SEM plan. Equally as important is a thorough evaluation of the current state of the institution through the examination of Strengths, Weaknesses,

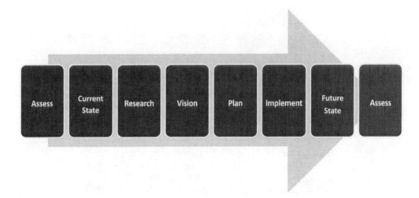

Figure 3.5   Lone Star SEM Infrastructure.

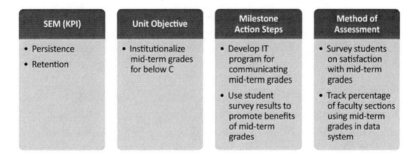

SEM (KPI)	Unit Objective	Milestone Action Steps	Method of Assessment
• Persistence • Retention	• Institutionalize mid-term grades for below C	• Develop IT program for communicating mid-term grades • Use student survey results to promote benefits of mid-term grades	• Survey students on satisfaction with mid-term grades • Track percentage of faculty sections using mid-term grades in data system

Figure 3.6   Lone Star SEM Strategies.

Opportunities, and Threats (SWOTs) and other data analyses. This examination should also include a review of technology, marketing, and all institutional processes.

Effective research allows the framing of the institution's desired future state, through the evaluation of best and promising practices and the removal of identified barriers to the enrollment and retention processes. Institutions should take time to explore the identification of resources and strategies for improvement as a new vision for the future state is established.

It is also imperative to continue to rally and engage stakeholders, as well as implement and evaluate stated goals and objectives through clear action steps and stakeholder ownership throughout the process.

To support and sustain SEM planning, monitoring and assessment, LSC imbedded the process into its Annual Cycle of Effectiveness (ACE) framework. This framework establishes that all LSC units engage in a process that involves developing and implementing plans for improvement and to actively assess the outcomes and effectiveness.

The framework prescribes that plans be identified, implemented, and evaluated. For SEM, this entails planning; identifying goals, objectives, and targets; determining action steps and ownership of activities; timelines and outcome measures (KPIs); implementing action steps; monitoring the progress of activities; and evaluating and assessing the impact of activities on outcome measures.

Accountability

Understanding the comprehensive nature of strategic enrollment management, the system office and college campuses committed to owning

parts of this robust process. The system office provided overall leadership in these distinct areas, including the planning process, support
in prospect and applicant yield, identifying enrollment opportunities,
and the development of SEM-related dashboards to allow campuses to
monitor and evaluate effectiveness.

The system office utilized data analytics, coordinated comprehensive outreach to Pell Grant recipients, conducted marketing, and
aligned SEM with LSC's ACE. LSC campuses assumed accountability
for scheduling/section management; development of campus-based
recruitment; enrollment and retention strategies; the development,
implementation and evaluation of campus strategies; coordination with
independent school districts; development of conversion strategies;
adherence to ACE, and establishing a campus-based SEM plan that
aligns with the systemwide SEM framework.

SEM Outcomes

As a result of the implementation of a comprehensive SEM process,
LSC was able to achieve several core outcomes. Broad campus engagement and inclusion were critical to the success of this effort. In addition
to the regularly scheduled meetings, the SEM Taskforce held additional
meetings with subcommittees, subcommittee chairs, LSC campuses,
and system office teams to allow for ongoing research and analysis and
measurement of specific outcomes, as identified below.

The following is a detailed roadmap of steps taken and outcomes
achieved during the time that I led these efforts at LSC. You may wish
to use a similar process or modify it, based on your unique culture and
environment.

The Process Roadmap:

1. Conducted SWOT analysis across the institution to identify
   Strengths, Weaknesses, Opportunities and Threats in business
   processes, systems, outreach, recruitment, enrollment, registration,
   retention efforts, and identified potential solutions.
2. Identified best practices in enrollment and retention at LSC campuses that can be replicated and scaled across the college.
3. Examined IT infrastructure and resources available to support and
   enhance enrollment and retention efforts.

4. Identified unique challenges for at-risk populations and used proven best practices to recommend interventions and supports.

5. Based on current research, identified which systems and processes might benefit by improved standardization and coordination, to yield greater impact on student success, retention, and completion across campuses.

6. Identified collegewide processes that will support and improve effective compliance with requirements of both the Department of Education and the Southern Association of Colleges and Schools Accreditation.

7. Identified and reinforced college and campus marketing strategies to support improvements in awareness, engagement, and enrollment.

8. Proposed a college communication and engagement process that integrated C-SEM strategies and proposed the utilization of the standardized council structures to ensure broad and efficient communication on campuses.

9. Proposed strategies to eliminate barriers to LSC's enrollment and retention processes to ensure student systems (i.e., recruiting, admissions, financial aid, advising, registration, billing and payments, scheduling, and student support operations) are efficient and student centered.

10. Recommended proven academic and social integration strategies and systems that support retention throughout the student life cycle.

11. Recommended tools to capture student feedback related to strategies, initiatives, and the overall student experience.

12. Produced reports and dashboards that help the committee easily digest complex data and inform data-driven decision-making.

13. Implemented an assessment cycle for the strategic enrollment management plan that monitors implementation of tasks, reviews the assessment of activities for continuous improvement, and utilizes analyses for planning future enrollment cycles.

14. Developed and implemented marketing strategies and technology enhancements that support the SEM implementation.

15. Researched, developed, and implemented SEM framework with the goals of championing the development and alignment of campus plans, reinforcing enrollment and retention and leveraging the data, analysis, strategies, and lessons learned from the Pathways Project,

which was designed to place students on track and reduce time to completion.

16. Completed collegewide SEM framework, Fall 2017—Fall 2020, which aligns key metrics by area and includes a Success Metrics Score Card to track progress.
17. Created resource repository, website, SharePoint, toolkit, data tools, dashboards, increased awareness, and better communication and workflow plans.
18. Enhanced student portal to include payment calculator to support flexible billing and payment plans and expanded outreach and communication to high schools and parents and faculty engagement in re-enrollment efforts.

RESULTS

LSC achieved a yield of increased enrollment of 52 percent, 50 percent, and 20 percent, for Spring 2017, Summer 2017, and Fall 2018 terms, respectively, as a result of the implementation of SEM strategies such as its Student Fast Pass, Targeted Recruitment, Re-enrollment, and SEM New Student Campaigns, representing the enrollment of 3,860 additional students and resulting in $15,440,000 of new revenue for Spring 2018. LSC also increased online enrollment by 14 percent between Spring 2017 and Fall 2018.

Reimagining and implementing a comprehensive strategic enrollment management plan will pay significant dividends in supporting the enrollment, retention, and graduation of students. It also builds a cohesive community committed to addressing current and projected enrollment challenges.

A LIVING DOCUMENT

In response to increasing competition, student diversity and the desire to improve retention, persistence, completion, and student success, it is imperative that colleges direct attention to shaping the entire student experience. Strategic enrollment management is a vehicle to examine all facets of the institution and their impact on student success.

The experience must be intentional and shaped to yield improved outcomes, from converting applicants to registrants, to reducing the numbers of students dropping out from one term to the next.

Colleges must consciously create new processes and procedures that support payment and redesign programs to establish services that are responsive to student needs, changing environmental factors and the anticipated enrollment fluctuations and potentially, the resulting reduced revenue generation.

Chapter 4

The Village Approach

Expanding Ownership for Strategic and SEM Planning and Outcomes

Collaboration is a key part of the success of any organization, executed through a clearly defined vision and mission and based on transparency and constant communication.

—Dinesh Paliwal, business executive

It is often said that "it takes a village" to raise a child. This African proverb means that everyone has a role in achieving the outcome of a healthy, happy child, one who is able to live up to his or her fullest potential.

A similar expectation can be set when developing strategic planning processes and achieving maximum outcomes. The approach requires intentional, inclusive, and expansive engagement with the college community and the community's commitment and ownership of the outcomes.

Every member of the college community has a role in the ultimate success of planning. Key to this success is open communication throughout both the planning and implementation processes. Equally as important is the effectiveness of leadership to ensure involvement of all areas throughout the institution.

It is critical that leaders bring together a cohesive and comprehensive ecosystem capable of supporting the planning, outreach, recruitment, enrollment, instruction, student services, retention, completion, and assessment functions. This cohesive planning infrastructure must also provide a flexible and seamless interchange that transparently interacts with the whole college community.

Colleges and universities are served best when cooperation and collaboration are clear expectations set at the initiation of all planning processes in order to ensure shared ownership of outcomes. When this occurs, the systems and strategies that emerge will best support operational and student success. An engaged college and university community is better able to design a transformational student experience.

Maya Angelou said, "At the end of the day, people won't remember what you said or did, they will remember how you made them feel." How our colleges and universities remove silos and barriers that prevent internal collaborations and create engagement opportunities across our campuses will make all the difference in ensuring that students feel connected and valued. It will create a culture that delivers a positive experience for everyone operating within our walls.

The ability to pivot with planning and approaches is important, yet we must remain uncompromising in our engagement of the entire community to establish confidence and goodwill. Our institutions must show that we care, that we listen, and that everyone in our village matters.

We must be deliberate in our commitment to expand inclusivity through transparency. College teams must work across the institution to map the student experience with a focus on learning and student success, above all other outcomes. Our teams must be willing to respect and acknowledge the unique contributions that each member of the community can make in support of this goal.

This approach to planning should also include redesigning current approaches to incorporate collaborative partnerships. Interdisciplinary and cross-college partnerships can be the source of innovative ideas. This approach also has been utilized successfully in the private sector through strategic alliances and partnerships that enhance institutional capacity to meet the demands of a new environment.

Peter Senge's learning organization work also centered on the value of cross-functional collaboration to increase effectiveness and meet environmental challenges. The National Institutes of Health and National Science Foundation have also espoused the importance and value of collaboration for knowledge creation and research, student learning, and improved organizational functioning.

Coordinating strategic planning and enrollment management planning across diverse multifunctional and multidisciplinary teams to solve complex institutional problems offers a clear advantage. By leveraging diverse talents and perspectives, institutions are better able to achieve innovative and shared outcomes in support of a collective mission.

Collaboration is a powerful vehicle. It can promote a dynamic institutional climate for learning and development for all of its members. The elements most beneficial to establishing a climate that cultivates collaborative teams are trust, communication, shared interests and goals, and clearly defined expectations.

In order to expand ownership of outcomes, there also must be a shared responsibility for planning. Consider adopting within your core values a commitment to excellence and accountability. A collegewide consensus about the importance of working collaboratively, buying in, and taking accountability for outcomes will enable a positive increase in internal partnerships and innovative discussions on change to emerge.

Colleges can achieve this by having (1) a shared vision; (2) visible and engaged leadership; (3) a clear charge and goals; (4) an agreed-upon mission, vision, core values, and strategy; (5) open engagement in the decision-making process; (6) the ability to listen; and (7) a willingness to compromise.

Incorporating each of these elements into the strategic planning process will lead to both tangible and intangible outcomes. Tangible outcomes can include joint development of goals, objectives, and strategies, and ultimately, the publication of the final plan with full college ownership and involvement in its development.

Design the plan to support the full implementation of new and revised programs and services, as well as a complete redesign of institutional approaches based on new priorities and strategic directions.

The opportunity to work with colleagues from across disciplines and departments helps to build stronger relationships and extends professional networks that continue beyond the strategic planning process. These trusted relationships stimulate the further emergence of new ideas and strategies supporting organizational connections, growth, and innovation.

Margaret J. Wheatley underscored the importance of human relationships and connections in *Finding Our Way*. She said that "Life needs to link with other life to form systems of relationships where all individuals are better supported by the system they have created."

These human capital strategies that engage the hearts and minds of faculty, staff, and students are likely to improve institutional climates, employee morale and positively influence outcomes and joint ownership.

THE ROLE OF CULTURE IN PLANNING

The Seventh Learning College Principle suggests that institutions should strive to "create and nurture an organizational culture that is both open and responsive to change and learning."

The effects of culture, whether positive, negative, or neutral, cannot go unconsidered and should not be ignored if the goal is the creation of successful internal partnerships and if institutions wish to have a transforming effect on its learners.

Culture is most frequently revealed through the relationships, attitudes, and actions of those within the community. A cultural change of this type will lead to more engaged college and university systems and positive connections by its members and others who come in contact with it.

Within collaborative environments, differences are recognized, appreciated, and celebrated due to higher levels of trust, cooperation, and inclusion. Strong internal partnerships within open and caring systems act as a catalyst for transformative change, as a result of the synthesis of ideas, equal access to power, group ownership of ideas, mutual trust and responsibility, respect and attention to process.

LESSONS LEARNED

- Collaborations can produce lasting benefits for institutions if the planning process is properly designed and managed.
- Creating conditions that encourage collaboration is an important way for higher education institutions to innovate and adapt in a time of rapid and continuous change.
- Internal collaboration requires all stakeholders, that is, administrators, faculty, staff, and students, to champion the process, to engage, and to invite others to participate.

A NEW WAY OF THINKING

Collaboration requires a stretch in institutional thinking. It strengthens your institution by connecting people, sharing knowledge and opportunities across departments, increasing internal competencies, leveraging specialization, and identifying needs and effective advocates.

Perhaps even more importantly, collaboration brings to the table viewpoints that would not normally be heard, given our traditional academic silos. Immediate outcomes of internal collaboration are increased efficiency and productivity. These are the results of streamlining processes and eliminating duplication of efforts.

It is critical that the goal of the collaborative effort be in alignment with the institution's mission and with participants' interests. The goal is communicated to stakeholders inclusively, widely across disciplines and traditional boundaries, with parameters for participation.

ONE COLLEGE'S APPROACH: METROPOLITAN STATE UNIVERSITY OF DENVER

Figure 4.1 shows the Metropolitan State University of Denver's Enrollment Command Center Structure. It is an excellent example of the creation of a cross-college collaboration to support the development, implementation, and measurement of enrollment management.

Metropolitan State University of Denver implemented the Enrollment Command Center (ECC) in spring of 2020 in response to the COVID-19 pandemic. It serves as an advisory committee to discuss enrollment strategies and to make recommendations that contribute to student access, recruitment, persistence, and completion during the COVID-19 pandemic and beyond.

This collegewide collaboration stays current on enrollment trends, data, and goals of the university to be as effective and intentional as possible, particularly during this unpredictable time. The model allows for the development of a holistic and integrated approach to enrollment management that supports collegewide collaboration, engagement, creative thinking, and consensus building.

It serves as a cross-functional hub to address challenges utilizing the talent of all team members. Enrollment management, like strategic planning, is viewed as a shared responsibility across the institution. All

Enrollment Command Center Structure

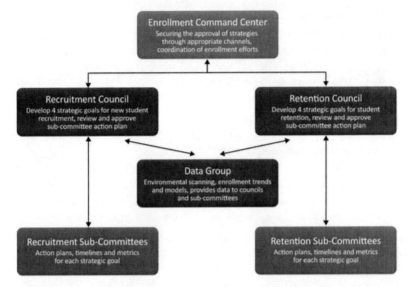

Figure 4.1 Metropolitan State University of Denver: Enrollment Command Center Structure. https://www.msudenver.edu/oem/strategicenrollmentmanagement/.

decision-making is supported and reinforced by the work of the Recruitment Council, Retention Council, and the Data Team.

Metropolitan State University of Denver Command Structure Goals:

- Increase engagement and strengthen collaboration in recruiting and retention strategies across the university.
- Revise and provide recommendations for student access, recruitment, persistence, and completion through diverse programs and services.
- Collaborate with university constituencies to develop, implement, and evaluate enrollment management goals and strategies that align while experiencing the pandemic.
- Share and disseminate enrollment information to recommend promising practices for enrollment.

This cross-functional hub created by Metropolitan State University of Denver is designed to provide enrollment management coordination and decision-making to support recruitment and retention efforts across the institution. It is one example of creating and sustaining a campus-wide culture for effective strategic enrollment management.

PLANNING FOR A NEW FUTURE

Shifting demographic and economic trends, funding decreases and state mandates have dramatically changed the enrollment landscape, such that many colleges are facing an uncertain future.

As one example, community colleges across the country are experiencing declining enrollments and one in ten community college presidents has expressed concern regarding institutional sustainability and the likelihood of merging or closing in the next five years.

New solutions are necessary, and these solutions will require greater collaboration and partnership, both internally and externally, if higher education is to thrive in the future.

It is critical to raise the standard and level of institutional planning. A truly reimagined SEM process must now develop and incorporate intentionally the focus on additional revenue streams. This addition may be the answer for a successful fiscal future that supports student and operational success. The bottom line is that, in order to maintain financial viability, colleges must evaluate all forces impacting enrollment, then prioritize and direct resources to efforts that make the biggest difference.

The consulting firm EAB, through its SEM research, suggested a Strategic Enrollment Management Plan Framework to assist in developing a holistic understanding of the enrollment environment. To be effective, the framework is goal-oriented, actionable, measurable, and aligned with institutional priorities. It provides directions on key steps of the planning process and recommends performance analyses, current and future market assessment, market and strategy prioritization, and a planning timeline.

The framework is designed to be used as an active document across the life of the strategic plan. In addition to assisting in developing a holistic understanding of the enrollment environment, the framework also assists in coordinating a collaborative approach to collegewide team building for the purposes of planning.

Through an inclusive and transparent process, a strategic vision can be built from available market analyses and demographic predictions. This will allow the emergence of a more transformational strategy that ensures the institution's long-term sustainability.

The three most important elements to creating a comprehensive and collaborative strategic enrollment management plan are (1) the ability to accurately analyze the forces shaping our current enrollment landscape; (2) effectively assessing the potential market segments to determine the return on investment; and (3) through open and responsive processes, engaging the college community in prioritizing both the low-hanging fruit (i.e., those strategies that will have an immediate return) and the high-return-on-investment opportunities that will achieve meeting enrollment targets.

Strategic enrollment management initiatives must be adopted as a shared responsibility that is also integrated within the academic ethos of our colleges and universities. We must connect the concepts of being academically driven and student centered.

ONE COLLEGE'S APPROACH: PITTSBURGH TECHNICAL COLLEGE

The institutional outcomes of being academically driven and student-centered can coexist within an applied and technical learning environment. Consider the experience of Pittsburgh Technical College (PTC), a private, regionally accredited, academically driven, and rigorous technical and applied college.

The quality of PTC's programs is demonstrated by a consistently high in-field placement rate (95 percent) and the success of alumni.

Two of the core values adopted by PTC are excellence and accountability. The college implemented a messaging strategy supporting this commitment, demonstrated by the motto of a "Higher Standard" and the tagline of "Where knowledge meets know-how." This messaging was adopted by every department and was defined by the PTC Magic, or the experience, provided to students and all who engage with the institution.

It is further demonstrated by each of PTC's academic schools and programs; from the School of Trades to the School of Information Systems and Technology; within certifications through bachelor programs; within the traditional face-to-face modality or within virtually excellent online instruction. Students earn stackable credentials, demonstrate strong academic ability in STEM and applied and technical competencies and are ready for professional careers immediately upon graduating.

In order to achieve continued success post-COVID-19, PTC's efforts to diversify its enrollment mix will continue through expansion of opportunities to enroll both traditional and nontraditional students. New strategies to attract and support underserved and underrepresented student groups, online students, adult learners, and veterans will increase. The college has redirected resources to hire additional staff to assist with specialized outreach to grow the enrollment of these populations. The college has committed to launching a Corporate College Department to secure alternative revenue streams through contractual training with business and industry, as well as other strategies.

EXPANDING PATHS TO ACCESS AND SUCCESS

Colleges can leverage student scholarships by aligning them with student outreach and recruitment priorities. Scholarships can build capacity for enrollment growth by also investing in innovative programs, instructional delivery techniques, and support to maximize student success.

As colleges and universities seek to expand access, it is equally important to ensure resources are directed at enabling the success of every student entering our doors. One proven strategy to support incoming students is to front-load student retention efforts within the first year, particularly in high-impact courses through such things as supplementary instruction and tutoring, learning communities, and mentoring programs.

The creation, implementation, and evaluation of innovative student services is critical. Establishing comprehensive student services that are responsive to student needs and exceed student expectations is also important.

Incorporating enrollment planning within the institution's strategic planning process will enable colleges and universities to build and sustain a SEM culture. Many institutions have adopted enrollment management strategies related to the administrative aspects of student recruitment, marketing, admissions, and retention. However, few have effectively aligned enrollment strategies with the priorities of the academic divisions through a collaborative model.

As enrollment challenges continue to intensify, additional cultural change will need to occur where shared responsibility for enrollment outcomes is an institutional imperative. We will need to reconsider traditional models across all aspects of our operations.

Many enrollment management experts have observed that few institutions have effectively designed and executed SEM plans due, at least in part, to an inability to foster a SEM culture and shared accountability for outcomes within the college community.

It is clear that enrollment planning is "strategic" when it is an integral component of institutionwide planning and resource management processes and aligned with the academic planning of our institutions.

To effectively anticipate and respond to the significant changes that affect college operations both pre- and post-COVID-19, leadership must effectively deploy strategic planning and management concepts in the blink of an eye to support innovative changes relative to our mission and values in a manner that assures institutionwide collaboration and ownership.

DEVELOPING A COMMUNITY

It takes a village to plan comprehensively, and the future success of colleges and universities will be determined by the degree of collaboration generated across the institution.

To establish the village concept, it is first necessary for everyone to see themselves as part of the same team, regardless of what position they hold or to what department they belong. The organizational direction will be determined by the institutional priorities and strategic directions.

As colleges develop strategic plans and enrollment strategies, it is critically important to also develop a detailed implementation and assessment strategy to assure the document achieves its intended aspirations and outcomes. If faculty and staff feel disconnected from the planning process and have not assumed ownership of its outcomes, the likelihood of the plan's success is minimal.

A plan must never feel as if it's a silo or a solo project; authentic involvement is key. In order for us to create a plan and culture that will enable our colleges to succeed, we must connect with and engage stakeholders throughout the institution, throughout the process. As the college community envisions its future, they will engage at a higher level with a greater commitment to listening, hearing, and appreciating diverse perspectives, while dreaming together.

MOVING FORWARD

Reimagined strategic enrollment management will enable a stronger re-emergence for higher education post-COVID-19, as SEM plans and practices expand access and opportunity. These plans must be comprehensive to effectively serve students, clearly identify goals, accurately measure success, and maximize institutional resources from entry to completion.

As higher education enters a new phase, post-COVID-19, the development of SEM plans should be learner-centered to enable the greatest level of success for a diverse student population.

The incorporation of market research and student feedback to guide decision-making and improve the overall teaching and learning environment, that is, removal of barriers and inclusion of additional wrap around services, will be critical. There may be an even greater need for counseling and advising supports in light of the traumatic impact that COVID-19 has had on families.

Institutions must conduct an in-depth examination of their current state in preparation for change. College and university leaders must evaluate strategic enrollment management plans and push beyond promoting an in-demand curricula to developing curricula that are delivered with greater flexibility, placing the learner first and backing all decisions with solid data to achieve intended outcomes.

Enrollment, demographics, and occupational data trends are helpful and provide a snapshot of the student body. Regional market data shine a light on the new student pipeline and target demands of an evolving workforce by anticipating what programmatic demands might emerge.

Additionally, competitive analyses can identify local and national competitors for program offerings and uncover new areas of opportunity while shaping the response of colleges and universities to market changes.

This comprehensive use of external and internal data combines to provide a comprehensive framework for decision-making and creates a web of important information and resources needed for a village approach and response.

THE BENEFITS OF A VILLAGE APPROACH

Within the village approach, there is a compelling vision and collective commitment to mission. Goals are developed and open discussions are had about the potential impact of decisions. Data is used to inform and focus discussions, frame priorities, and align plans with intended outcomes. Organizational capacity and the active solicitation of diverse ideas from throughout the college community is a priority.

Most importantly, a greater focus on the institution's future is revealed as silos are removed, people authentically engaged and greater ownership in the planning process and its outcomes are attained. As inclusion and transparency are increased and increased levels of trust develop, stakeholders are able to become truly engaged in meaningful change.

Planning is about people, collective hopes and aspirations, and core values and principles. At its best, planning reveals what people can contribute, what matters to them, and ultimately, what they want the institution to become.

One activity that helped Pittsburgh Technical College expand its village approach was an invitation to the college community to participate in ongoing discussions about a vision for the future.

The entire college community was invited to engage in a variety of strategic visioning exercises. Many joined the college leadership for a vision walk around the 185-acre campus to discuss what they envisioned. Leadership's role was to listen, hear, and connect the dots as an expanded vision for the college unfolded.

What dreams did they dare to dream about PTC? What might the institution become in the next five years or decade? I'm proud to say that, as president and chief dreamer of Pittsburgh Technical College, a new level of engagement emerged that day. A college community dreamed together about new possibilities that they would create. As college leaders, we must engage our community of dreamers—we must make room for their dreams, and we must incorporate the power of their transformative ideas into our planning to shape the future.

Chapter 5

Adding Revenue Diversification to Balance the Enrollment Picture

Balance is not something you find, it's something that you create.

—Jana Kingsford, Big Dreams Coach

The need for colleges and universities to achieve financial viability by broadening revenue is becoming one of the most critical issues facing higher education at this unprecedented time.

The COVID-19 pandemic helped to curtail revenue streams for higher education. With Fiscal Year 2021–2022 enrollment and auxiliary revenues uncertain, many leaders are looking for alternative revenue opportunities to support ongoing operating costs and emerging expenses.

Institutions continue to face significant challenges resulting from declining funding levels, enrollment shifts, increased competition, rising costs and demands for heightened accountability from families and other stakeholders. Many are incorporating diversified revenue streams to offset these challenges. New and innovative revenue diversification strategies are emerging to finance missions and balance the enrollment picture.

Establishing supplemental revenue streams from a variety of non-enrollment sources is essential for long-term survival. Expansion in areas such as continuing education, credit and noncredit certificates, degree completion and programmatic upgrades, study abroad, domestic and international branch campuses, distance education, auxiliary services, technology transfer and partnerships, and alliances with other organizations are key examples of some of the directions being taken. These activities are integral to lasting and responsible financial strategic planning.

Institutions are incorporating more entrepreneurial approaches to address decreasing enrollment revenue, reduced resources, dwindling infrastructure, and shifting levels of financial support. The addition of new revenue streams helps to secure the future during periods of uncertain enrollment. Nontraditional income sources are fast becoming an increasing method of funding for some colleges and universities.

Without the benefit of these alternative or additional revenue streams, more colleges will be forced to make decisions to cut programs, lay off personnel, and/or even merge with other schools. Some may even face the loss of accreditation or be forced to close as a result of financial pressures.

Small private colleges face an even greater challenge, as higher education plans for a future where expenses might potentially outpace revenue and where tapping into endowments to cover shortfalls or higher rates of tuition is a limited or nonexistent option. Moody predicted that the growth in operating expenses will eventually outpace revenues at most institutions. Moody further suggests that a 3 percent growth in revenue would be needed for most colleges to remain financially stable.

The current environment calls for colleges to set a course for strategically addressing enrollment dependency by developing institutional priorities and strategic directions that will lead to the development of opportunities to expand revenue.

PITTSBURGH TECHNICAL COLLEGE'S APPROACH

In its strategic plan, Pittsburgh Technical College developed six strategic priorities, four of which focused directly or indirectly on improving institutional financial sustainability. Strategic Directions 1, 3, 4, and 5 each supported financial growth.

The figure 8.1 on page 80 displays the strategic directions that guided the Pittsburgh Technical College's strategic planning planning process. A more detailed discussion will follow later in this book.

Strategic Direction 1 moved the institution to expand access to broader student groups. This direction led to developing strategies to expand outreach to targeted student groups through local school districts, interagency connections, faith-based organizations, and veteran groups.

Strategic Direction 3 intensified the focus on aligning the college's curriculum with workforce demand. This enabled PTC to expand opportunities to work with business and industry partners to grow internship and apprenticeship opportunities, as well as coordinate post-graduation placement.

This also will allow for new opportunities to provide training and development to the more than 300 business and industry partners serving on the Pittsburgh Technical College Advisory Boards and to support the 2022 launch of the PTC Corporate College.

Strategic Direction 4 supports the elevation of public and private partnerships and guides the college's focus on innovative funding opportunities through grants, foundations, and philanthropic resources.

Strategic Direction 5 maintains focus on the overall need for financial sustainability and stewardship and led to increased efficiency measures and transparent and inclusionary budgeting practices.

THE FINANCIAL VIABILITY FORECAST

In a survey conducted by *Inside Higher Education*, only 44 percent of chief financial officers felt confident that their institutions would remain financially stable over the next ten years. This is down from 54 percent in 2016. Building financial viability by broadening and diversifying the funding base through alternative streams of revenue may make it possible for colleges and universities to reset financial trajectories to deliver on their missions and drive excellence in a sustainable way.

There are important benefits to higher education casting a wide and innovative net to pursue new and diverse revenue sources. Revenue diversification enables institutions to generate additional income and secure additional resources and discretionary finances to improve the teaching and learning environment, hire the best faculty and staff and provide a safety net of wrap-around services to a diverse student population.

Enrollment generates approximately 80 percent of college and university income. In order to improve challenges with long-term financial sustainability and projected decreases in enrollment, colleges and universities should consider incorporating strategies for alternative revenue generation to successfully scale existing activities and reduce excessive dependency on enrollment as their primary source of revenue.

Diversifying revenue streams beyond enrollment in traditional face-to-face classes by expanding online programs and commercializing facilities, among other innovative strategies, may generate promising institutional revenue.

Another important strategy for improving the financial health of the organization is to drive operating efficiencies by reducing costs. The most common option is to target personnel costs, which typically represent approximately 50 percent of the operating budget.

OPPORTUNITIES TO EXPAND
REVENUE GENERATION

A strategic focus on revenue diversification will offer colleges and universities the opportunity to not only acquire additional revenue but also to expand internal innovative collaborations. Examples of alternate revenue sources for colleges and universities are limited only by the creativity of the institution.

Strategic advancement of online and virtual education and training, continuing education programs, evening and weekend programmatic offerings, and facilities usage year-round for collegiate and community engagement and learning are a few examples of what some colleges have done in the area of alternative revenue generation.

Other examples also include the incorporation of in-service, short-term and tailored training programs. Colleges and universities also have launched collaborations to attract new financial resources, such as expansion into commercial and business fields, as well as contracted research, training, and consultancy services.

There is an increasing demand from both public and private organizations to upgrade the professional skills of the workforce, which presents further opportunities to generate revenue through training programs.

What follows is a brief list of specific institutional examples of revenue diversification.

- Unity College, a small, liberal arts school, determined that generating additional revenue is a critical strategy for reducing the cost of tuition. Looking internally, the college found campus farms to be a resource to increase revenue.

  This allows Unity College to provide students both an education and real-life experience in the farm industry. The college produces income by growing, harvesting, and selling produce and livestock to local markets, restaurants, and the general public.
- The integration of technical or business incubators at colleges and universities is also gaining in popularity as an alternate stream of institutional revenue. Incubators are being launched across a variety of industries and disciplines to support industry and college partnerships, creative think tanks and internships and apprenticeships. Wayne State University created an incubator known as Tech Town. The venture raised a total of $3,964,627 for the university in 2016.
- At the Johns Hopkins University's Applied Physics Laboratory, researchers developed a prosthetic arm that is controlled by the user's brain. It is still undergoing a variety of tests with patients; however, the lab has begun to identify collaborations with industry partners to bring the technology to market.
- Franklin Pierce, a small university located in Rindge, NH, revived the college's political polling operation in 2016 to generate income and help the college's reputation and brand. In addition to the revenue generated, Franklin Pierce received free publicity and brand recognition, leading to almost double the number of undergraduate applications.

Other ideas to consider:

- Immersive workforce-ready professional programs that represent short and targeted boot camps are focused on improving student employability in specific disciplines. The number of students graduating from these boot-camps in the United States has grown considerably, from 2,178 in 2013 to 23,043 in 2019.
- Alternative digital credentials refer to online courses outside of degree programs and include credit-bearing micro-credentials, which may "stack" to attain a degree. This model is growing steadily. Moody's found that one in four U.S. colleges now offers digital skills

badges, and 73 percent state that alternative credentials are "strategically important to their future."
- Education brokering for employers is an opportunity through an employer partnership to deliver higher education for current employees. Across the United States, 35 percent of the university population is over twenty-four years of age. This segment is expected to grow much faster than the number of students aged eighteen to twenty-four. Educational brokering will enable colleges and universities to train and retool the incumbent workforce.

The following leading global universities successfully have applied revenue diversification initiatives to support institutional sustainability:

- A leading U.S. university used a continuing education model to set up a professional education team focused on building partnerships with corporate and government training divisions. Over the past five years, the university has collaborated with more than fifty companies.
- Utilizing research and innovation as their approach to revenue generation, the University of Michigan in 2007 established a Business Engagement Center (BEC) as a way for faculty to partner with business leaders across a variety of fields.

  The BEC maintains ongoing partnerships with more than 1,200 companies. It has contributed to a 53 percent increase in corporate philanthropy and a 163 percent increase in corporate research expenditures.
- The University of Chicago not only rents its premises but also assists in event planning. This approach to asset utilization is a successful revenue-generation opportunity for colleges and universities.
- The University of Pennsylvania launched a cobranded credit card to its alumni in 1997 through Bank of America, the benefits of which include cash back on various purchases, no annual fee and a low annual percentage rate for the first twelve months.

  Additional revenue is generated through a revenue-sharing agreement in which Bank of America contributes a percentage of funds to the university with every account opened and with every purchase made using the cobranded card.

IDENTIFYING NEW OPPORTUNITIES

As a result of the challenges brought on by the COVID-19 pandemic, new opportunities are emerging to develop coventures. Two recent examples include a college engineering lab that combined its efforts with healthcare professionals and used an array of 3-D printers to manufacture face shields, and three different colleges collaborated with a major healthcare organization to re-engineer ventilators for faster and less expensive manufacturing.

Customized academic programming and training is one of the most requested avenues that can serve to support alternative revenue generation. Providing training in employee recruiting and onboarding, executive leadership and management within the virtual space, supply chain security and logistics and webinars, among other educational trainings, may provide an opportunity for growth in this area.

STEPS IN REVENUE DIVERSIFICATION PLANNING

As you determine a plan for revenue diversification and identify potential revenue streams for your institution, the following steps might also prove helpful:

1. First, establish a cross-functional team to explore and develop a plan for diversification. There should be agreement on the approach and key priorities.
2. Conduct an in-depth analysis of what areas across the college might represent immediate opportunities for success. Develop a list, placing those with greatest impact and least investment first. All areas should align with the college's strategic plan and support the mission, vision, and core values of the institution.
3. Lastly, it will be critical to develop a plan of action with clear strategies for initiating, maintaining, and evaluating. This actionable implementation roadmap must be championed with clear accountability and leadership.

Many colleges adopt a revenue diversification portfolio approach when embarking on this path. The diversification portfolio identifies several revenue alternatives with varying degrees of risk and revenue potential. Areas are selected that can deliver short-term wins, and these successes are used to generate momentum and support.

The most amazing ideas can emerge from anywhere in the organization, so it is important to create an open and inclusive community where opportunities for dreaming, creativity, and entrepreneurial thinking are nurtured.

The need and importance for institutions to strategically seek innovative alternative streams of revenue post-COVID-19 will continue to grow. Identifying alternative streams of revenue will take an investment of time and resources, but the return on that investment may prove well worth it.

Chapter 6

Leading Strategic Planning to Maximize Engagement and Financial Sustainability

Strategic planning does not deal with future decisions, it deals with the futurity of present decisions.

—Peter Drucker, management consultant, educator, and writer

A reimagined strategic planning process is critical for reinvigorating and transforming college and university planning efforts. The more inclusive and transparent the process, the greater the chances for long-term momentum and success. A clear communication and engagement strategy will be critical to reinforcing the actions and attitudes needed to achieve results.

The planning process and the strategic plan should be supported by the college community. Its ultimate success will depend on many members of the community, and therefore, they should have knowledge of the plan, its direction, and through a coordinated process, share in the accountability for its development, implementation, and evaluation. Without this level of expected engagement, it will be difficult to accomplish the plan's priorities, vision, and goals.

The planning process should be designed to maximize the talents existing within the college community, and given the current higher education landscape, the plan should also support institutional growth and financial sustainability.

The process must allow for the creative exchange of ideas, a safe place to explore, innovate, and align ideas with a shared vision that leads to solutions to current or projected challenges. It is important to understand the market in which your institution operates and the opportunities it presents in order to determine how to best focus your institution's unique strengths. Colleges and universities should be clear on the current state of the institution.

Those leading the process must be committed to the organization's core values, possess the knowledge needed to execute the process, and demonstrate the skills and abilities to garner trust and accountability for the results.

The strategic planning process and plan can also serve to position colleges and universities comprehensively to achieve greater organizational success. This is achieved through heightened internal and external collaborations and partnerships, which serve to identify and fill operational gaps through a highly engaged and inclusive process.

PLANNING TO PLAN

Critiquing the Previous Plan

A comprehensive assessment of the most recent strategic plan is a critical component and should be undergone prior to launching the process for developing the new one.

During this assessment process, it is important to review the goals and strategies of the previous plan. This review should consider if any unachieved goals and objectives align with the new strategic vision and institutional priorities. If so, it must be determined if they should be transferred into the new strategic plan.

A good strategic plan includes specific, short-term goals covering all the areas that need improving in order to attain the vision. The goals must be measurable and concrete. The strategic plan should delegate responsibility for each goal to a specific individual at the college.

The Visioning and Planning Process

Vision is essential. Colleges and universities will not advance in any direction without it.

Visions should be long-term, ambitious goals. Examples could be to become the educator of choice, to overtake the current industry leader, or to implement a nationally recognized corporate college model. The strategic vision gives the destination, but it is the strategic plan that maps out how to get there. Through the strategic visioning process, leaders should examine the college's mission and clearly define its purpose and the unique role it plays in the higher education landscape.

Moving forward to fulfill that mission and purpose requires colleges to first look back at history and around at the current environment, then determine goals and how to move forward to realize them. The exercise requires drilling down to reach a granular level of information. It requires seeking and hearing the perspective of various constituent groups, both internal and external to your organization.

With insight, the team can begin strategic visioning—believing in the ability to realize big dreams by paving a path with a well-defined mission, sound strategy, and clear direction.

Conducting a strategic visioning activity is helpful in igniting the planning process and allowing those serving on the strategic planning taskforce and other members of the college community to envision what possibilities might unfold.

Transformative Planning

It is clear that the pandemic's economic and social impact might serve to accelerate transformational change in higher education, forcing critical attention to innovating around enrollment and programmatic changes, and identifying, in more intentional ways, new revenue and cost-cutting or efficiency measures.

There is no more important time than now to engage in effective strategic planning as colleges and universities seek to preserve dwindling resources, increase flexibility, and the ability to pivot and test new approaches to address emerging challenges. This unique moment in time provides an opportunity to become stronger through continuing evolution.

A transformative strategic planning process involves the use of an environmental scan to examine market trends, federal and state budget allocations, consumer preferences, and competitor behavior. This allows scenario building to consider potential changes in college and or in the behaviors of students, families, community, competitors, funders, and other stakeholders.

The constant, rapid changes in higher education require greater focus and adaptability from colleges and universities and those that lead them.

It is essential that as colleges develop strategic plans, they incorporate more agile business models and contingency plans that take into consideration what has been learned during the response to COVID-19. Leaders must reflect and envision beyond the pandemic to the new markets and jobs emerging, projected trends and consider scenarios regarding higher education's longer-term survival. It is at that time they can best institute a process to develop a strategic plan that will reposition its core operations for sustainability and long-term growth.

PLANNING FOR CHANGES IN THE FINANCIAL LANDSCAPE

During the realignment of strategic planning to maximize engagement and financial sustainability, substantial resource shifts may occur in order to address declines in enrollment and operating revenues, and as another result of the pandemic, potential concerns associated refunding of student payments.

This period in higher education has brought declines in endowment values and the risks associated with debt covenants and short-term bond refinancing, paving the way for the need to re-envision strategic planning. Huron Consulting in its December 2020 publication suggested that this period could offer an opportunity to stabilize financial operations by shifting resources and developing cash flow projections.

Additionally, engaging larger numbers of campus constituents in decision-making and execution will allow stabilization to take hold, as colleges and universities reduce spending and modify policies to support readjustment. Building a framework into the strategic plan that allows for the evaluation of debt capacity, and the evaluation of such things as endowment liquidity will set the stage for further transformation.

Implementing a comprehensive and inclusive strategic planning process will further position colleges for change and long-term success. It should be supported by an integrated budget and an innovative financial planning model that aligns with the intended outcomes and goals of the plan. This can be supported by the use of appropriate reporting tools with forecasting capabilities, allowing for projections, as well as enabling the evaluation of programmatic and operational effectiveness.

Chapter 7

Integrating a Framework for Change to Guide Results

Change is inevitable, but transformation is by conscious choice.

—Heather Ash Amara, author and motivational speaker

College and university leaders are adept at responding to varying levels of change. One of our most important roles is to anticipate and recognize change in order to help those within the college community respond strategically.

The COVID-19 pandemic made it abundantly clear that we cannot predict or control for all change, but we must gather our wits quickly and respond. Institutions must learn to navigate through periods of uncertainty. These periods provide lessons that can guide and shape future actions. Change is constant, and institutions must use it to ignite transformation, in order to thrive.

The change of this moment has forced colleges and universities to alter operations and transition from one state to another. This change generated increased concern, fear, and loss of control across the higher education landscape. All across America, COVID-19 forced colleges and universities to quickly switch, many for the first time, from brick-and-mortar education to virtual learning.

As COVID-19 continues to spread its effects throughout our country and our lives, campus administrators everywhere are unsure what lies ahead. No matter the answer to this question, it will require a reimagining, and it will be the task of higher education leaders to find the opportunities hidden within the chaos. As Jose' Saramago wrote, "Chaos is order yet undeciphered."

This period of massive change has created the opportunity for colleges and universities to think differently about the work of higher education. How will higher education respond and lead through this period, keeping our organizations focused and moving forward? How will we reckon with the demand for immediate change, fewer resources, and an even higher level of scrutiny and accountability? How will our structures and missions evolve to better align with the needs of those we serve and gain increased relevance with business and industry as new jobs emerge?

Institutions will be served well by integrating a framework for change to effectively guide results. It will also require bold and competent leadership, comprehensive and integrated communication strategies, increased collaboration, and compassion.

During this period, visionary and entrepreneurial leadership will make the difference. As colleges work through this period of change and uncertainty, we must seize this moment to reimagine and create innovative partnerships, expand research, development, and training for jobs of the future, ensure professional development of faculty and college teams, redistribute the higher education infrastructure, and launch more innovative curriculum post-COVID19.

What has become abundantly clear is that a chance has been provided for higher education leaders to redefine our future by design and our role in it. Providers of rigorous education and training for the middle-skilled workforce have a unique opportunity—in fact, the responsibility—to take a leadership role in rebuilding our communities, states, and nation, upon emergence from this global pandemic.

The ability for colleges and universities to be nimble and pivot on a dime will be essential, and those with a focus on technical and applied careers may have an added advantage. Through effective leadership, change management and planning, technical and applied colleges and universities will find a welcome home in the new normal. As employment expediency becomes even more critical, their curriculum will be the preferred curriculum due to its alignment with business and industry. These institutions understand the emerging needs of employers as they prepare students for tomorrow's jobs today.

There is limited clarity on the long-term effects of COVID-19 on the workforce. What we do know is that the needs of employers will be different. We can anticipate that different ways of working will emerge, a differently trained workforce will be required, and organizations will need to reexamine strategies for change and transformation.

To do so requires understanding how workforce needs are changing and gaining that understanding requires listening to employers and elevating public and private discourse and partnerships.

When the current crisis abates, our region, our nation, and our world are going to need to rebuild. New technologies and associated jobs will be emerging, and employers will want the credibility and proven skills that come with having the appropriate certification and degree. Colleges and universities must be ready to educate students with the knowledge and skills to succeed in the workforce. Their ability to succeed will only be heightened by the ability to adapt quickly to changing circumstances.

ADAPTING TO INNOVATE

Change management is a systematic approach that colleges and universities can use to respond to change, adapt to change, and effect change. It allows for defining and implementing procedures or technologies to deal with changes in the environment.

Successful adaptation to change is crucial within an organization. The more effectively people and organizations deal with change, the more successful and stable they will become.

Important components of change management models are the creation of strategies for effective communication and identifying potential areas of resistance so that it can be reduced or eliminated. Change management is an ongoing process that requires time, expertise, and commitment to implement, and as a result, these models often lead to a higher return on investment (ROI).

Successful change management requires the involvement of a broad range of institutional stakeholders in order to align strategies with the needs of the college and university, for a smooth transition from its current to its future state.

Change management allows colleges and universities to assess the need and impact of change, align resources, reduce resistance, and provide strategies for the execution of an effective communication strategy to improve collaboration.

The added efficiency with which institutions are able to respond to challenges and the improved success rate of change efforts are important benefits to incorporating effective change management models.

While there have been repeated calls for educational change and reform in higher education, greater clarity on change management is critical at this time. Institutional leaders must understand the change process and how these models can assist. Understanding and utilizing change models will help institutions communicate, plan, implement, measure, and evaluate efforts.

COVID-19 has forced considerable change and provided an opportunity to better explore change processes. As colleges prepare to enter a new phase of evolution, the use of systemic change plans guided by theory, research, and best and promising practices will help them better understand the forces that drive change, give insight into faculty and staff reactions, and enable the development of a change management framework.

As educators repeatedly address change in response to the needs of students, faculty, and the broader community, operations are altered in reaction to these external and internal forces of change. Institutional change may be the result of new leadership, new economic realities, technological breakthroughs, competition, community or political influences, or any number of events impacting the organization.

The change theories, as articulated by Hossler (1990) and subsequently by Kotter (1995) and Owen (2001), are particularly helpful during this period of massive disruption in higher education, as a result of the potential of an enrollment-related financial crisis.

For educational change to be successful, the external and internal forces of change must be assessed, monitored, and evaluated to reduce or avoid the impact of threats to effective change and to determine the strengths and weaknesses of the institution as it encounters significant change (Fullan, 1999).

Bringing about fundamental change is sometimes very difficult for many organizations and bringing about transformation can be almost impossible. This is especially true in organizations that are as highly bureaucratic as institutions of higher education. For example, the units within these institutions, specifically student affairs and academic affairs, often work as a house divided, when it comes to making changes in support of student learning and development. Colleges and universities cannot continue to work within any paradigm that is counterproductive to the change process. These silos cannot remain and must be collapsed into a seamless learner-centered system.

CHANGE MANAGEMENT MODELS

An educational change management model is a schematic description or diagram of a system, theory, or phenomenon that helps make sense of educational and organizational change. It gives structure and meaning to an administrator dealing with change-related problems, enables effective communication of ideas, and helps with the visualization of the big picture of change by breaking it down into smaller, more manageable parts.

The understanding and integration of change management models is critical for transforming higher education post-COVID-19. These models will support the institutional adaptation to change during this unprecedented period in American higher education.

There are several exceptional change models that can be referenced to support this important work. Below are three of the more popular models as well as an original model to support organizational transformation.

Kotter's Change Management Model

Kotter's Change Management Model has eight stages and focuses attention on the organization's response to change, preparing for change, as well as change implementation. This is one of the most commonly used change management models.

The first stage of Kotter's Model is the focus on increasing a sense of urgency for change. This serves to motivate and engage members of the college community during the change process, (Kotter, 1996).

The next two stages (Build a Guiding Coalition and Form a Strategic Vision and Initiatives) involve building a team that will drive change

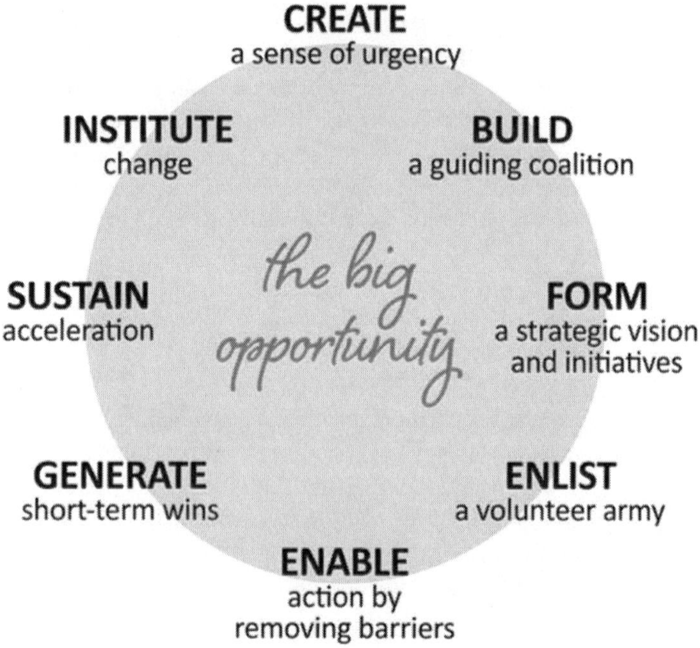

CREATE
a sense of urgency

INSTITUTE   **BUILD**
change   a guiding coalition

SUSTAIN   *the big*   **FORM**
acceleration   *opportunity*   a strategic vision
                                and initiatives

GENERATE   **ENLIST**
short-term wins   a volunteer army

ENABLE
action by
removing barriers

Figure 7.1   Kotter's Change Management Model. From G. P. Kotter's *Leading Change*, 1996.

and align a supportive vision that considers the creativity and passion of those within the organization. The next stage (Enlisting Volunteer Army) calls for uniting people around a shared vision.

Stage Five (Enable Action by Removing Barriers) seeks to expand capacity through extensive communication in a transparent manner and enable further action by removing barriers and roadblocks to change, while collecting feedback to measure progress.

Stages Six (Generate Short-Term Wins) and Seven (Sustain Acceleration) in Kotter's Model focus on celebrating the short-term goals that have been achieved, in order to encourage continued progress and incorporating and sustaining change by reinforcing it as part of the workplace culture.

Stage Eight (Institute Change) is a critical element of the model and addresses the need to anchor change within the culture for long-term sustainability.

McKinsey 7-S Change Management Model

The McKinsey 7-S Change Management Model is another popular framework and is one of the longest-lasting organizational change management models. This model consists of seven categories that are important for colleges and universities to consider when implementing and addressing change. Unlike many change models, the McKinsey 7-S Model focuses on a wider variety of factors that may impact success.

McKinsey's model is a reminder of all the business aspects that should be defined before the change strategy is implemented.

The 7-S Change Model offers the following important elements to consider:

- Strategy, step-by-step plan to build competitive edge
- Structure of organization
- Systems used to complete daily operations
- Style, manner change is adopted or implemented
- Staff, workforce, and working capabilities

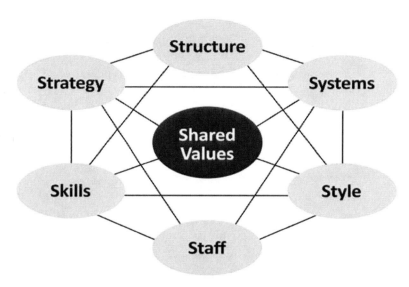

Figure 7.2   McKinsey 7-S Change Management Model. From Waterman, Peters, and Phillips's "Structure is not organization" in *Business Horizons*, vol. 23, no. 3 (1980); reprinted with permission from Elsevier.

- Skills or competencies possessed by employees
- Shared values, to which college or university is committed

Lewin's Change Management Theory

Lewin's Change Theory provides a popular approach to understanding change management. The theory describes change in three distinct and continuous stages impacting: pre-change, change, and post-change.

Due to its simplicity, many organizations have utilized Lewin's 1947 theory as a concise framework for change implementation. The theory opined by Lewin, and adapted below, clarifies transitional change in organizations by unfreezing and preparing for change, transforming, and refreezing, where change and transformation solidifies.

Unfreeze is the preparation stage for change and involves strategically addressing organizational resistance in order to melt and ready the culture to shift and reshape. The most critical step at this stage is leadership and communication. The goal is overcoming resistance to planned change and improving change responsiveness.

The Change stage is where transformation is implemented throughout the organization and new structures, systems, practices, and processes

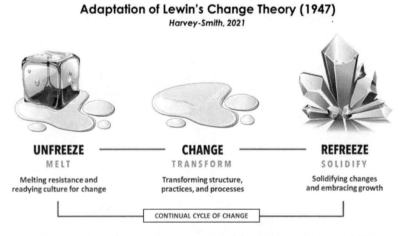

Adaptation of Lewin's Change Theory (1947)
Harvey-Smith, 2021

UNFREEZE ——————— **CHANGE** ——————— **REFREEZE**

MELT   TRANSFORM   SOLIDIFY

Melting resistance and   Transforming structure,   Solidifying changes
readying culture for change   practices, and processes   and embracing growth

CONTINUAL CYCLE OF CHANGE

Figure 7.3   Lewin's Change Management Model. Based on Lewin's *Field Theory in Social Science: Selected Theoretical Papers* (EdD Cartwright), 1951.

take form. This stage builds onto the first stage of melting resistance, and good leadership and effective communication remain crucial.

The last stage, Refreeze, is where change solidifies and is accepted by a critical mass of the organization. During Refreeze, transformations and new expectations are integrated into the culture. As routines settle and the organization stagnates, the cycle of change repeats.

Harvey-Smith's Three-Stage–Ten-Step Change Model

Harvey-Smith's Three-Stage–Ten-Step Change Model represents a framework that emerged from extensive research across multiple institutions, exploring the adoption of innovation and change.

The research study *The Adoption of the Learning College Paradigm in Vanguard Community Colleges* also gave birth to the Seventh Learning College Principle, which guides colleges and universities to "create and nurture organizational cultures that are open and responsive to change and learning." This reinforces the importance of organizational culture to successful and transformational change efforts.

The three stages of the model are *prepare*, *innovate*, and *sustain*, as noted in the detailed model below.

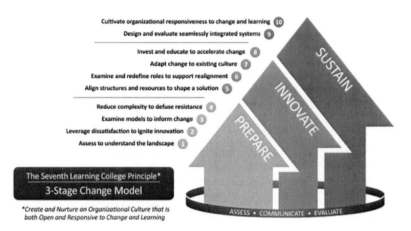

Figure 7.4   Harvey-Smith's Three-Stage, Ten-Step Change Model.

Stage 1: Prepare

Before acting, it is important to assess. Determine the change that is being perceived and what is preventing adoption of and/or causing resistance. During this stage, you may also want to explore existing models to support reduction of change resistance.

As you develop ideas for meaningful change, keep things simple by presenting concepts in gradual, absorbable chunks—even if behind the scenes you are building a complex apparatus to support successful change.

Train your leaders as conduits for change. Nurture your teams and incorporate their suggestions as much as possible. Keep the lines of communication open to whittle away resistance and build genuine buy-in.

Stage 2: Innovate

Once a path for transforming the organization has been carved out, it is time to realign your structure to achieve those outcomes.

Create opportunities for uniting organizational silos to gain efficiencies and spark synergies. Map out how individual roles need to be adjusted or cross-trained to support new approaches and interrelationships.

Remain sensitive to the established culture and how changes can best be adapted to any long-standing values and norms. Develop and implement policies, training programs and communication protocols that strengthen team member understanding and transformation.

Stage 3: Sustain

As challenging as it may be to launch organizational change, momentum will quickly falter without continual follow-up and refinement. Establish accountability at all levels by designing evaluation measures and checkpoints. Get input on the changes, plug any holes, adjust processes, and recognize improvements and stellar performance.

Demonstrate that you are committed to the transformation and guide its diffusion into the organizational culture. Foster a learning-centered environment and agile responsiveness to continual change and growth.

Ten Steps

Step One: Assess the Current State

This first step consists of assessing the current state to gain understanding before proceeding. This can be achieved in a variety of ways, including an in-depth SWOT analysis to gather information from internal and external stakeholders.

Step Two: Leverage Dissatisfaction to Ignite Innovation

This step flows from the assessment process. If there is significant dissatisfaction, it confirms the need for change. This level of dissatisfaction can be leveraged to ignite momentum and launch the change process. It can also serve as a critical driver toward innovation and transformational change.

Step Three: Examine Models to Inform Change

Step Three guides organizations to examine models of best and promising practice to inform change. Institutions may create or adapt viable models to improve outcomes in existing structures. These models set parameters that will influence stakeholder engagement, change implementation, and provide a level of predictability.

Step Four: Reduce Complexity to Defuse Resistance

Step Four is best represented by the need to strategically reduce complexity and resistance to change by separating large-scale change initiatives into smaller more understandable components. Change complexity and resistance can also be reduced through the utilization of effective communication strategies, which authentically and transparently discuss change and its need for integration.

Step Five: Align Structures and Resources to Shape a Solution

Step Five urges the strategic alignment of organizational structures into the infrastructure and networks needed to successfully achieve the goals and objectives identified in institutional change initiatives. This step also calls for the alignment of resources with specific changes to support positive outcomes.

Step Six: Examine and Redefine Roles to Support Realignment

Step Six provides the opportunity for colleges and organizations to respond to organizational stagnation by evaluating and redefining organizational roles in support of the evolving needs of students and the transforming organization.

Step Seven: Adapt Change to Existing Culture

Step Eight: Invest and Educate to Accelerate Change

Emerging naturally from redefining and realigning organizational roles is the need to adapt and anchor change and transformation into the organizational culture. Steps Seven and Eight call for investing in capital and human resources to include change education. Educating the community through strategic communication and alignment of organizational processes, systems, programs, policies, and services can accelerate change.

Step Nine: Design and Evaluate Seamlessly Integrated Systems

Step Ten: Cultivate Organizational Responsiveness to Change and Learning

Steps Nine and Ten address the need to strategically design and evaluate change processes and systems. This is done to assure the comprehensive and seamless integration into the organizational structure and system. Step Ten drives attention to the need to also actively cultivate a responsive organizational culture that supports ongoing change and transformation.

A CASE FOR URGENCY

The need for colleges and universities to utilize some form of change management model and approach is important to accelerate change and will impact the rate at which they will be able to respond to challenges successfully. The ability to respond and adapt to change quickly is essential and a matter of urgency for colleges and universities as higher education continues to adjust to current and future disruptions.

Chapter 8

A Case Study

Aligning Strategic Directions to Achieve Institutional Priorities

> *Continuity of strategic direction and continuous improvement in how you do things are absolutely consistent with each other. In fact, they're mutually reinforcing.*

> —Michael Porter, academician

Colleges and universities typically measure success based on the achievement of mission-critical outcomes. For institutions of higher education, effective planning and alignment with critical priorities can lead to sustained impact. Concurrently, the institution must monitor its internal environment, assess external opportunities and threats, and revise its strategy in response to change.

Developing an effective strategy and coupling it with specific actions will translate into the likelihood of greater success. In order to achieve institutional priorities, institutions should align strategic directions targeted to achieve outcomes. It might also prove helpful to consider the following critical questions:

1. Does the institution have the right personnel with the appropriate skill sets to achieve the stated outcomes?
2. Does the current institutional infrastructure support the targeted goals and objectives?
3. How might programs and services be changed to support emerging markets?

4. Are additional strategies and resources needed to support organizational sustainability?
5. Does the organizational culture support the effective implementation of the strategic priorities?
6. Are the strategic directions aligned to achieve the institutional priorities as stated?

Moving from strategy development to implementation, strengthening staff and faculty capacity, elevating collaborations and partnerships, aligning strategic directions to support institutional priorities, and building leadership effectiveness are all crucial to a successful planning process.

PUTTING IT ALL TOGETHER

An Abbreviated Case Study: Pittsburgh Technical College

Pittsburgh Technical College (PTC) developed a unique strategic planning framework that supported and reflected its specific needs and culture. Through this case study, the PTC story is presented with important lessons learned through the strategic change process that can apply to any college or university undertaking similar work.

Organizational Background

A private, nonprofit college located southwest of Pittsburgh, PA, on a scenic 185-acre campus, Pittsburgh Technical College opened in 1946. Formerly Pittsburgh Technical Institute (PTI), the college was an employee-owned, for-profit school until 2017.

Pittsburgh Technical College has since expanded to offer more than thirty programs in traditional, hybrid, and online formats across eleven academic schools.

Pittsburgh Technical College Schools of Study:

• School of Trades and Technology
• School of Business
• School of Criminal Justice
• School of Culinary Arts
• School of Design and Engineering Technology

- School of Energy and Electronics Technology
- School of Healthcare
- School of Hospitality
- School of Information Systems and Technology
- School of Nursing
- School of Online Studies

PTC is institutionally accredited by the Middle States Commission on Higher Education and is authorized by the Pennsylvania Department of Education to award Certifications, Associate in Science and Bachelor of Science degrees.

There are five buildings on campus, including a six-story main facility that serves as the primary site for instruction. The main building also contains classrooms, labs, a large gallery and meeting places, professional kitchens on the sixth floor for culinary students, a bookstore, the PTC Café, lounge areas, and admissions and financial aid. The Trades and Technology Center houses the School of Trades Technology and Energy and Electronics Technology Programs. Approximately 51 percent of the student population lives in school-sponsored, apartment-style housing, both on campus and at complexes in neighborhoods surrounding the campus.

PTC is set apart by its unique and innovative delivery of high-demand academic and workforce programs, along with an explicit focus on student outcomes and placement. This commitment to effective education and real-world preparation of students is demonstrated in a placement rate of 95 percent for PTC's 2018 graduates working full-time, part-time, or freelance in their field.

Evolving and Envisioning the Future

The college continues to innovatively evolve and define its path forward. Programs at PTC have earned the following specialized accreditations and designations:

- Surgical Technology: Commission on Accreditation of Allied Health Education Programs (CAAHEP), Accreditation Review Council on Education in Surgical Technology, and Surgical Assisting (ARC/STSA)
- Medical Assisting: Commission on Accreditation of Allied Health Education Programs (CAAHEP) and Medical Assisting Education Review Board (MAERB)

- Practical Nursing: Accreditation Commission for Education in Nursing
- Practical Nursing and Associate in Science Nursing: Pennsylvania State Board of Nursing
- Therapeutic Massage Practitioner: National Certification Board for Therapeutic Massage and Bodywork (NCBTMB)
- Associate in Science degree and certificate program in Culinary Arts: American Culinary Federation (ACF)
- Information Technology: National Center of Academic Excellence in Cyber Defense Two-Year Education (CAE-2Y) through the National Security Agency (NSA) and the Department of Homeland Security (DHS)

Strategic Planning: Position of Strength

Pittsburgh Technical College embarked upon its strategic planning process from a position of strength. Several factors motivated PTC to engage in an in-depth strategic planning process to address immediate and projected challenges.

PTC is celebrating its seventy-fifth anniversary in 2021/2022. This historic milestone coincides with the conclusion of its current strategic plan and its recent hiring of a new president, a recognized higher education leader, to serve as the first president to lead since acquiring nonprofit status.

The selection of a new president/CEO provided the opportunity to engage in comprehensive strategic visioning with multidisciplinary, cross-functional teams to develop transformative strategies, structure, and culture to ensure processes aligned with a vision of success for the future of the organization.

New Leadership

Upon arrival, the new president introduced three institutional priorities and a series of well-researched strategic directions to drive momentum.

This set the stage for the college's future evolution by leveraging this transformational period, reimagining the institution, and implementing an innovative strategic planning process to write the next chapter. The planning process allowed for the development of a five-year plan, which included the hiring of key cabinet members to support sustained change.

The president implemented an intentional and unique hybrid approach to senior leadership at the cabinet level, combining the skills and expertise in for-profit and nonprofit educational leadership, in an effort to combine the best ideas from both industries, supporting a collective and innovative vision for Pittsburgh Technical College.

Leadership transition, opportunities for growth, desire for greater financial sustainability, need for additional revenue streams, changes in accreditation status, new name, and other organizational changes and milestones like the college's first presidential inauguration and seventy-fifth anniversary, provided major momentum and served as the impetus for a tremendous change effort. This effort allowed the college to fully engage and reimagine its future. The convergence of these occurrences also created the opportunity to answer these key questions:

- Who are we as a newly accredited nonprofit college?
- What do these changes represent?
- How might we leverage our new name and new president to reintroduce the college to the community?
- What do we want to accomplish?
- How do we stabilize the organization and grow?
- How can we become a thought leader in this space?
- How do we build a culture of excellence and accountability?

All of these questions stimulated a commitment to strategic planning and galvanized the college around a collective vision.

Invitation to Engage

The president extended an invitation to the entire college community to engage in the planning process, to examine market impact, and to explore the strengths, weaknesses, opportunities, and threats that existed.

The president made the conscious decision not to hire a consultant but to lead the college through the strategic planning process herself. All members of the President's Cabinet played an active role in supporting this critical process. The vice president of Academic Affairs played an important role in facilitating team discussions. Members of the President's Cabinet were also involved in critical elements of the process. Additionally, the board of trustees was actively engaged throughout the plan's development and provided feedback.

The president and all members of the taskforce modeled inclusive decision-making and ensured that decisions were sound, that they leveraged PTC's competitive advantage and that the organization was aligned behind the strategic vision and six strategic directions as illustrated in figure 8.1 to achieve the institutional priorities.

Integrated throughout the process was an intentional focus on the role that organizational culture plays in successfully delivering on strategic priorities. These strategic directions were the focus of interdisciplinary strategic planning work groups. Each strategic direction was cochaired by two individuals to assure the teams were adequately supported.

The Strategic Planning Taskforce and Strategic Direction Subcommittees provided regular updates to the college community, which provided feedback to shape the final plan.

Figure 8.1 Pittsburgh Technical College's 2020–2025 Institutional Priorities and Strategic Directions.

An Insider's View

At Pittsburgh Technical College, Strategic Direction 6: *Promote Culture of Excellence and Accountability*, served as the connective tissue through each strategic direction and provided a window into the college's perception of how the organization operates, as well as an opportunity to share thoughts about change and change resistance.

This gave clarity to the leadership, enabling them to avoid blind spots and operating on false assumptions about staff and board perceptions. Discussions of organizational identity, market and competitive advantage, and the assessment of the organization's culture were completed early in the process.

In addition to conducting a SWOT analysis, the organizational culture was further assessed through surveys conducted by Top Workplaces issued by the *Pittsburgh Post-Gazette* and Energage Consulting, as well as internal employee satisfaction and student satisfaction surveys.

Armed with a better understanding of culture and with the full engagement of the college community, PTC was able to develop strategies and plans for implementation that included the type of culture development needed for organizational success.

PTC wanted additional clarity about strategies to be explored, tested, aligned, and put into practice throughout the organization and regularly engaged the college board, management team, staff and key partners, and stakeholders to resource and deliver on these strategies.

As the following timeline figure shows, the process allowed a deep dive into conversations about past successes and failures as a means to design a strategy for the future. Each meeting and discussion was designed to build upon the last and to support reflection, discussion, and planning (Harvey-Smith & Steffan, 2019).

This further allowed clarity regarding the intended outcomes of the planning process. PTC built its process to yield several outcomes. Through the process, the college desired to:

- Be in a stronger position to serve as a thought leader in the space, it occupies through recognition of the talent and expertise at the college
- Be in a position of strength to successfully achieve its mission through greater understanding of the external environment in which it operates and through agreement on and confirmation of key strategies to respond to this environment

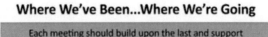

Figure 8.2 Timeline and Direction.

- Gain greater clarity about the current state and culture of the college and an enhanced focus on planning for its desired or future state, its priority work, issues, challenges, and opportunities
- Build stronger teams by reducing or eliminating silos that prevent effective internal collaboration and partnerships in pursuit of institutional excellence
- Clarify the college's understanding of its unique strengths and organizational identity and how these support its strategic decision-making
- Identify an organizational structure that is aligned with carrying out its strategies and will enable it to successfully achieve its mission through the strategic directions
- Develop clear guidance for how the organization will make ongoing decisions aligned with organizational strategies
- Increase the skills and capacity of organizational leaders, staff, and board to make ongoing strategic decisions, enabling the college to respond to changes over time

A Solid Foundation

Ultimately, the goal of every strategy development project is to create a foundation for success and to align the organization to build on that foundation. To this end, the PTC teams framed their work as having the following phases:

- Understanding the strengths, weaknesses, threats, and opportunities that exist for the college
- Examining models of best and promising practices for strategic planning and goal development

- Developing and confirming their strategic goals and objectives in alignment with each strategic direction in support of institutional priorities
- Developing plans to translate these strategies into operational plans
- Implementing plans successfully to create maximum impact and assess

Through this framing, the process also delivered on one of the key outcomes identified by the board: a clear and consistent understanding of PTC's core identity and organizational strategy.

In navigating this trajectory, everyone throughout the organization understood overall direction and reasons why resources were focused on specific areas of work. The president engaged the entire board and staff in this process and used it as an opportunity to also identify and build the skills of staff leaders throughout the organization.

The teams worked tirelessly in achievement of a collective vision throughout the COVID-19 pandemic. The committee guided and shaped the process to ensure it would produce the outcomes needed.

Timeline for Success

It was important to set a clear timeline for when the work of the Strategic Planning Taskforce and Strategic Direction Subcommittees would begin, this included ground rules and expected operational protocols. The need to balance the work and to celebrate successes was also extremely important.

This proved very successful for Pittsburgh Technical College, as work continued on schedule throughout the COVID-19 pandemic, with the final strategic plan receiving full board approval on schedule for the intended launch.

The following figure identifies the period for preliminary preparation and the strategic direction roll out that proceeded the formal planning process.

The Process

Over a one-year period of planning, the faculty, staff, and board, through a series of facilitated discussions, considered both existing opportunities to strengthen the organization's impact, as well as evolving needs.

Figure 8.3   Strategic Direction Rollout.

The process used to develop and discuss the ongoing nuances of the strategic plan with the college community were transparent, inclusive, and focused on strategic directions in alignment with institutional priorities.

PTC used both the small and large group engagement of the six strategic directions teams, individual team discussions, and ad hoc subcommittees, as necessary. Each team was highly encouraged to conduct research, draw conclusions, and make recommendations to the broader body. The larger team defined as the Strategic Visioning and Planning Team met monthly for reports and discussions. The Strategic Directions teams met more regularly, at least two times per month.

A variety of resources were provided to support planning efforts and included:

- The college's prior strategic plan and sample plans from high-performing institutions
- An environmental scan
- An institutional profile
- Demographic and budgetary summaries
- Access to conduct recommended research

It was essential to engage the college community in planning and building for the future through collective engagement and emotional investment. Among the many benefits of this approach were the following:

- Improving leadership and management skills for the faculty and staff who served as leads for the strategic direction subcommittees
- Creating a healthy environment for open and honest input, feedback, and debate
- Expanding members' total organizational perspective by breaking down functional silos
- Helping all employees work together closely, gaining empathy for the various departments, operating for the overall good of PTC

A great quote from Pat Summitt, legendary women's basketball coach from the University of Tennessee, summed this up well: "Responsibility equals accountability equals ownership. And a sense of ownership is the most powerful weapon a team or organization can have."

As PTC moved into a visioning and strategic planning discussion, the first part of the activity was "Heads Up" and was meant to draw out the dream of the team. The second part of the meeting was "Sleeves Up" and was intended to focus energy on a real-world strategy that would achieve the dream. The exercise was designed to be fast-paced, highly interactive, and visually oriented.

Daring to Dream

Throughout the planning, teams were asked to reflect on the past, assess the current state, envision the future state, and develop clear and measurable goals to move the college in the direction of the future state.

As a critical part of the strategic planning process, PTC redefined its vision and reviewed both the institution's mission and core values prior to delving into identification of goals and objectives aligned with the strategic directions.

The strategic vision was a concept of PTC's future that was used to shape the business strategy. Combining the vision with a solid living plan made it real for the organization to achieve. The vision defined what the institution imagined PTC becoming: its future growth, the caliber of employees, and values.

To stimulate the team's ability to envision beyond the current state, they were asked to answer the question: "What do I really want for PTC? Describe what you see as the ideal in your mind's eye, using a statement that begins with 'I see . . .'"

For example, "I see PTC as setting the benchmark of effectiveness and efficiency in all operations in an effort to promote the stability needed to realize the highest standards of student success, performance and profitability."

PTC desires to rank among the best private, nonprofit colleges in the nation in technical education. In order to achieve this, based on the current state, the college needed a plan to help grow in positive recognition.

Once the institution knew the current state with clarity, the team developed a plan to begin the journey to take the college forward, including identifying the needed improvements.

Goals and Objectives

The leadership for implementing the goals and objectives for each of the strategic directions was aligned with a member of the President's Cabinet and core teams who are accountable for championing efforts and measuring outcomes.

The goals and objectives also were supported by the full Strategic Planning Taskforce and the Strategic Direction Subcommittees.

The goals and objectives are reviewed as a regular component of the President's Cabinet meeting, college staff meetings, and board meetings to assure it remains a living document.

Monitoring Progress

The president supported prioritizing and approval of strategies to be implemented. Planning and monitoring tools were also developed and implemented to support the plan's full implementation. An important function of this role is the identification and mapping of strategies and their alignment with each strategic direction implementation.

Assigning responsibility for PTC's plan also meant establishing ongoing measurements and milestones. If a milestone is missed, the progress is reviewed to determine what went wrong.

Preparing to Launch

In keeping with this goal, the Strategic Planning Taskforce, comprised of cabinet members, board liaison, senior staff, faculty, and other staff leaders, launched Phase 1 in December 2019 and Phase 2 in January 2020.

The PTC Board Strategic Committee also engages with ongoing review and discussion of the plan. The overarching leadership of the strategic plan implementation was constructed to use cabinet members as leaders for each strategic direction.

Each served as the primary functional lead for the objectives and strategies under a functionally aligned strategic direction. Throughout the planning and implementation process, additional individuals with specific functional expertise and oversight for specific strategies were added. By having cabinet members and functional/strategic direction leaders serve as implementation leads, the teams are able to provide progress updates at regular cabinet meetings.

The plan, vision, mission, and core values are reviewed regularly with formal revisions as needed. Changes in the higher education landscape and throughout the institutional environment are examined and may require a revision to the strategic plan. Changes in competition, technology, or staff are key triggers that may necessitate a change in plan.

There is significant benefit to broad involvement in the strategic planning and implementation process. The following are comments from the multidisciplinary, cross-functional Strategic Planning Taskforce about their involvement in the strategic planning process.

PTC Community's Reflection on Process

"Assisting with the development and process means I will also have an impact on the results. That's meaningful to me."—Denise Fisher, Director, Financial Aid Planning

"Helping others who have not been involved in this process before gave me a great sense of community."—Jeff Leedstrom, former Director, Admissions

"Creating the plan allows us to set the goals. Setting the goals allows us to envision the future of PTC!"—Jay Clayton, Vice President, Administration, and Chief Finance Officer

"The cross-departmental collaboration during this process has been wonderful. It's been very enlightening to work with folks that have different perspectives."—Bill Showers, Chief Information Officer

"There are about 5,000 colleges and universities in the United States. We are all confronting the same problems. The difference at PTC is that we are nice to each other while we solve them."—Keith Merlino, Associate Vice President, Student Services

"No fear! We were free to state our opinions in a professional manner, without fear of censure or ridicule. Our team followed that principle, and the result was very effective meetings. My personal belief is the results our team achieved were directly related to our ability to discuss any topic."—Dave Becker, Chair, School of Energy and Electronics

"The president arrived with a vision. On Day One, she provided key priorities and strategic directions to move the institution forward. The strategic directions set a solid vision for the future, the college's growth and aligned with previous discussions. A clear pathway to PTC's future was set, and the entire college community was engaged to make it happen.

"The president invited us to be authentically involved in figuring out the 'HOW.' That was the difference—she did not present a plan, she presented a vision, and we were able to create the plan.

"With previous strategic plans, the plan was created, and we were simply given it to carry out. Very few people were involved in the planning process. As a member of the senior leadership team, I was aware, possibly more than most in the community, and even I didn't feel a sense of ownership with the last plan. This time it was very different.

"In the process that was led and modeled by our new president, a main focus was inclusion and ownership. It became *our* plan. Dr. Harvey-Smith invited anyone who wanted to serve on the strategic planning committee to step up and be a part of the process. Nearly seventy people stepped forward to serve—nearly a third of our community.

"The president provided the strategic directions, but it was with her guidance and the work of the Strategic Direction Subcommittees that further defined the directions and created the objectives and strategies. The strategic planning process provided me and the cabinet with an amazing professional development opportunity.

"I was able to work closely with the president throughout the coordination of the strategic planning process. She is an amazing and generous teacher and leader. She listened to my ideas, guided me and shared a wealth of resources. Serving with her to lead the strategic planning process is one of my greatest professional experiences. I am excited to start the implementation process.

"My good fortune includes having several wonderful mentors who have influenced my professional growth and career path over the past 40 years. In a very short time, my president has become one of my most influential mentors. She is not only changing PTC (the institution), she is changing every person within the institution, and I put myself at the top of the list.

"The strategic planning process actually started during the recruitment of our new president by the college and Board of Trustees. They identified a candidate who could bring the vision and strategy needed to transition and transform PTC into a new era. Never in the history of the college had the development of a robust strategic plan been more urgently needed.

"Before she even accepted or started in her new position, our soon to be president saw the potential in PTC, and it was that potential she saw that moved her to accept the role. She knew that with her vision and the potential for the college, PTC could achieve greatness.

"Before beginning her role, she researched and investigated the college to identify possible next steps. She took the opportunity to form the Key Institutional Priorities and Strategic Directions. Prior to accepting the position, she conducted in-depth conversations and sincerely invited feedback from the board and PTC leadership about the proposed Institutional Priorities and Strategic Directions to ensure leadership alignment.

"As a result, the president was able to hit the ground running when she started by laying out for all stakeholders of the college her vision, priorities and directions."

Eileen Steffan, EdD
Vice President, Academic Affairs

Pittsburgh Technical College's vice president of marketing and communication, Barry Shepard, had this to say about the process and leadership involved in strategic planning:

"The president felt it critical to communicate with and engage our broader community. She very effectively communicated to the faculty and staff. She coined the term, 'PTC Magic' to describe the experience that we can provide through our culture. She emphasized that with our amazing underlying 'Magic' and the targeted priorities and directions, that we could all accomplish something very special together.

"The president had credibility from Day One from all stakeholders, so there was immediate buy in to the vision, which became our collective vision and ultimately our strategic plan. She wanted to ensure that the strategic plan process had ownership from the faculty and staff . . . well beyond buy-in."

"The president was adamant that we would *not* involve outside consultants, but rather all of us would participate in the creation and nurturance of our plan. That was mission critical for not only buy-in but also the accountability, not for just developing the plan, but for achieving the execution and results over the next five years."

"The highly inclusive process allowed for a second level of leadership to emerge and execute with excellence. We were encouraged to step out of our comfort zones and normal roles to take on an added responsibility."

Presidential Reflections

In the course of developing our strategic plan, we have been able to change culture while implementing a process to impact the full academic community for years to come. Joining Pittsburgh Technical College at the onset of developing a new five-year strategic plan proved to be an exciting opportunity.

Together, we set the course for the future and reimagined PTC's next chapter. Through an open and transparent process, the college was invited to dream with me and to imagine a future by our design. Together, a brave team of dreamers began a year-long process of crafting our path forward.

As president, I had the pleasure of working with and getting to know nearly seventy individuals, inclusive of all PTC departments, who committed themselves to serving on the Strategic Planning Taskforce and thoughtfully framed this critical plan, assuring that it represents the shared goals of our community.

In 2020, COVID-19 brought unique challenges for higher education that forced unexpected change and the need for strategic reflection, planning, and subsequent execution. Across the educational landscape, the coronavirus pandemic shifted enrollment, interrupted educational plans, reshaped employment, and significantly impacted instructional modalities.

Pittsburgh Technical College was technologically well prepared to close its campus for several months to protect the health and safety of our community, maintaining education in a fully virtual environment.

In July 2020, we strategically reemerged, poised to transform the educational ecosystem, student experience, and teaching and learning environment to embrace a new normal. This process also gave birth to an extensive Return to Campus Plan, which served as a precursor to the strategic plan.

We are now virtually excellent in the online environment and have expanded our fully online programs and student support services to academically and socially engage learners.

While the full impact of the coronavirus on education remains to be seen, I am confident that PTC is positioned to make decisions that will result in a higher standard for education in our region, state, and nation.

PTC is a unique organization, blurring the boundaries between what is considered traditional technical training and college education. We are the future of higher education. Our innovative approaches are being incorporated by our peers, and we strive to continue to lead on a path toward revolutionizing academia.

With a precise focus on student success and the future, we will continue to create and nurture an organizational culture that is both open and responsive to change and learning, as I wrote in the *Seventh Learning College Principle*.

Our strategic plan is a living document and a testament to the college's evolution and growth as a higher education institution committed to operational and student success.

The challenges of 2020 have provided a renewed vision, expanded mission, and clear values that will lead us to broader inclusivity.

We believe our strategic directions of expand access, enable success, align workforce demand and curriculum focus, elevate public and private partnerships, enhance financial sustainability and stewardship, and promote culture of excellence and accountability, capture the beauty of our dreams, and will help us to create a sustainable future.

Through continued planning, the alignment of institutional practices with student and organizational success, the seamless integration of systems, and a reinvigorated culture will serve to elevate Pittsburgh Technical College.

We emerged from the planning process believing in our key priorities of becoming an educator of choice, a primary pathway for filling middle skills jobs, and fueling economic development to rebuild our commonwealth, and serve as a model for other educational institutions.

Pittsburgh Technical College will expand its work with business and industry and educational partners to meet the ever-changing needs of students and employers.

We will strive to maintain or exceed our consistent 95 percent in-field placement rate, of which we are so proud. We also will grow our relationships with governmental and philanthropic constituents who illuminate our mission.

PTC's strategic plan reflects the college's engagement with a broad array of talented internal and thoughtful external stakeholders about the future of education, the future of work, and the future of Pittsburgh Technical College.

The Next Chapter

As we plan for the next chapter, as defined within our plan, our dreams, and actions will align and present tremendous opportunities. Our culture will embrace and celebrate creativity, as the transformational power of education seeds renewed hope.

Pittsburgh Technical College's key priorities and strategic directions will guide tactical planning and budgeting practices. We will make steady progress and will integrate a brilliant mix of applied and technical education with rigorous academic requirements. This is the cornerstone on which our work must be built.

The success or failure of an organization is heavily weighted on the leaders who serve and their ability to learn from the past and anticipate the future and act. To achieve the outcomes within our strategic plan, we set the following three leadership goals in alignment with our priorities and strategic directions to drive our continued planning and execution:

• Empower the faculty, staff, and students of Pittsburgh Technical College to seize every opportunity to bring their best self to every situation. We will work smart and ground every action and interaction in excellence.
• Enhance transformational teaching practices, learning, and work environments and embrace cultural competence in fulfillment of our

core values. Quality interactions with the college community must be grounded in compassion, appreciation, respect, and empowerment.

• Invest in our employees, creating an innovative, empowered workforce that is given the tools and opportunities to think bigger and better about everything we do.

It will be important to provide opportunities for all employees to be heard, to engage, to grow professionally, and to enhance and apply the intellectual capital, knowledge, and skills necessary to achieve institutional priorities and strategic directions and goals. This is key to institutional success and means that PTC aims to be student- and learning-focused as we evolve and live our pledge to be a higher standard now and in the years to come.

LESSONS LEARNED AT-A-GLANCE

1. Organizational identity and competitive advantage are foundational building blocks when developing a strategic vision.
2. Organizational culture is critical to any change process and its ultimate success. Create and nurture an organizational culture that is open and responsive to change and learning.
3. Explicit decision-making criteria can enhance rapid adaptability.
4. Strategic clarity paves the way for aligning new staff behind strategic goals.
5. Organizational leadership must be champions of the change process by articulating and modeling its value.
6. Reaching agreement on a process to guide decision-making can accelerate how organizations respond and adapt to changes in a dynamic environment.
7. Developing a sound strategy that leverages its competitive advantages and organizational capacity can help determine whether the pursuit of certain opportunities will ultimately strengthen impact.
8. Engaging the college community in change leadership strengthens the willingness and ability to sustain change.
9. Presidential leadership for change is essential and engaging the President's Cabinet in strategy development and implementation can reinvigorate the change and strategic planning process.

10. Opening the strategic planning process to engage the broadest involvement will build momentum and buy-in for transformational change.

Balancing deep staff engagement in strategy development and implementation planning requires ongoing attention and nurturing. Prioritizing staff involvement in these processes can often overwhelm staff, as the demands of participation may compete with the demands of daily accountabilities.

Clarity regarding expectations and roles can help maintain a more effective balance. This is what PTC sought to achieve by engaging staff in planning and implementation teams, and explicitly articulating the roles and importance of these teams.

It is my hope that this case study helps to illuminate the critical link between the open and transparent processes and the broad engagement needed to develop a sound strategic plan and implementation process.

It is offered to inform and inspire colleges and universities to re-engage and reimagine their planning efforts by effectively aligning strategic directions to achieve institutional priorities.

The institution has evolved throughout its seventy-five-year history, and it continues to do so today, aggressively positioning itself to meet the challenges and opportunities of a changing higher education landscape. Developing this degree of adaptability from a position of strength is but the latest chapter in the Pittsburgh Technical College story.

Chapter 9

Key Strategies for Repositioning Institutions for Increased Effectiveness

Strategy without tactics is the slowest route to victory, tactics without strategy is the noise before defeat.

—Sun Tsu, ancient Chinese military strategist

Tuition costs continue to increase, while retention and graduation rates trend downward; colleges and universities across the country are at an inflection point as increasing calls for accountability mount. The response will require a comprehensive reexamination of institutional effectiveness from student entry to completion, as well as a general examination of all operations.

The time for higher education to keep promises made to students and their families about long-term student success and workforce preparation is now. No longer is it acceptable nor practical to manage the system of higher education as a revolving door, with far too many students entering and leaving with mounting debt, no degree, and no clear career path.

In order to transform the educational experience and outcomes, it is necessary to strategically reposition approaches to develop new solutions to the challenges that continue to plague higher education.

Colleges and universities are encouraged to shift practices to improve their success serving a broader, more diverse student population, create alternative streams of revenue, and build an institutional culture that is open and more responsive to change and learning in order to sustain.

SHIFTING LANDSCAPE

As the landscape continues to change post-COVID-19, the survival of higher education will depend upon its commitment to reinvent itself in response to the massive disruption it has experienced. This will encompass a repositioning in thinking, planning, and execution to address new and evolving expectations.

Effectively repositioning higher education for the challenges that lie ahead will require cultivating college leadership that is inspiring, entrepreneurial, and caring, with a strategic vision and courage to lead boldly.

Leaders must have a strategic vision capable of galvanizing the college community to dream big, while readying the institution's culture for the diffusion and adoption of innovation.

Caring leadership is transformational. It results in the emergence of more highly effective organizations. Being able to empathize and display high levels of emotional intelligence and to see yourself in others can be a powerful tool. The research and definitions of leadership are extensive. Peter Drucker pointed out that leadership is doing the right things.

In doing the right things, effective leaders must authentically care about others. Moreover, an example of a significant contribution to leadership effectiveness is the concept of CARE. It represents, essential leadership standards as identified in the following figure.

CARE is the essence of exceptional leadership and separates good leaders from great ones. It is difficult to be an effective leader, if one lacks compassion, appreciation, and respect for others or does not understand the importance of empowering others through a collective vision (Harvey-Smith, 2003).

Leaders who demonstrate "care" recognize that central to their success and that of the organization is the ability to help others succeed. This concept grew out of research on high-performing institutions, and how they effectively repositioned themselves by adopting new paradigms and transformed practices to achieve greater outcomes.

The study further endorsed redirecting greater attention to higher levels of organizational engagement and supported the establishment of an environment that values and integrates the voices of its members into planning and seeks to inspire peak performance. These actions can serve as drivers for organizational success at a fundamental level.

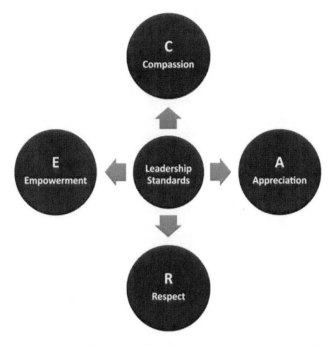

Figure 9.1 Harvey-Smith's Essential Leadership Standards: CARE Model.

REPOSITIONING FOR SUCCESS

As colleges and universities reposition for greater success and effectiveness, leaders must envision the possibilities by dreaming big, planning strategically, and acting with intention. This involves focusing on the institution's capacity for change in all areas.

It entails the development of a plan of action utilizing the talents of the broadest number of community members to yield the likelihood of success as initiatives are launched. The level of engagement and buy-in to the planning process will expand the reach and impact of strategies.

Most importantly, acting with intention will allow colleges to be courageous in the execution of strategy. The CARE model empowers leaders to take risks. Armed with a bold and collective vision, colleges will achieve great things, as innovative partnerships and internal collaborations emerge to drive effective change.

Incremental efforts yielding minimal impact must be abandoned, as colleges answer the clarion call for transformative change. Repositioning institutions for increased effectiveness will mean a departure from past practice.

It will mean exploring every facet of the operation and intentionally redesigning new ways to operate, including evaluating systems and processes, clarifying goals, and assessing outcomes. Colleges and universities must make courageous shifts in curriculum design, support services, instructional approaches, financial models, and personnel.

It also means examining recruitment, retention, completion, and placement rates to improve overall operations and outcomes. Colleges and universities are further encouraged to align both planning and practice with the community's broader needs, while building a pipeline supporting a clear pathway to the future.

Tenacity and grit will be needed to focus on the institution's broad vision and mission with clarity for successful repositioning, while identifying priorities and strategies.

ENVISIONING THE FUTURE

Any vision for the future must align with a plan for long-term sustainability and be implemented transparently to allow the college community to engage in determining the "how" strategy and goal development. This will make an important difference in the success and buy-in to internal and external repositioning strategies.

Rethinking scheduling and teaching practices to address the changing needs of students is also important, as the interest in both part-time and online offerings is increasing. Expanding the availability of evening and weekend classes and programs to accommodate the number of students who work full-time and may wish to pursue higher education at a more nontraditional pace is worth considering.

As the number of low-income, first-generation, underprepared, and nontraditional students with gaps in their educational experiences increases, the need to expand financial assistance and availability of comprehensive wrap-around services will be even more critical, post-COVID-19 to position students and institutions for heightened success.

Higher education must continue its move from the sage-on-the-stage or lecture-based model as its primary instructional methodology to incorporate more innovative teaching strategies in response to diverse student learning styles.

The utilization of technology to collect and analyze student data is a necessary strategy. Through analytics, colleges and universities can assess competencies and redesign curriculum.

Along with offering part-time learning opportunities, colleges and universities may want to consider the integration of competency-based education, providing students greater control and motivation for their role in the learning process.

Implementing structured pathways is another strategy; it reduces time to completion by providing a plan at entry and removes courses that are less critical to the student's academic goals. The academic plan supports structure and reduces costs.

The following strategies provide additional food for thought as colleges and universities focus on repositioning for improved effectiveness and success.

ADDITIONAL REPOSITIONING CONSIDERATIONS

While all colleges and universities may operate differently in some ways, there are still elements which are consistent across institutions. For example, a common vision remains critically important for all institutional types. It is therefore, important that the institution's leadership, faculty, and staff all commit to a common vision. A vision that embraces student and operational excellence, enables the comprehensive integration of targeted strategies and the effective prioritization of both strategies and outcomes to achieve institutional priorities.

The integration of these strategies will provide greater efficiency and reduce the likelihood of duplication of effort, as well as provide an opportunity to clarify priorities and connections for faculty, staff, and other stakeholders.

Recognizing that the college infrastructure plays a vital role in the institution's ability to achieve its outcomes, it is important to examine the organizational structure and infrastructure, to include a comprehensive assessment of its physical space and IT infrastructure. This assures the institution's capability to deliver on its promises of student learning and operational success.

Build a culture of evidence and inquiry that permeates the institution. Continuously examine experiences, the progression, and the outcomes reached by students, faculty, and staff and utilize the analyses to create, implement, and evaluate strategies for improvement.

Disaggregated data will enable colleges to gain greater clarity and understanding of the various student groups they serve and better support and monitor the progress of traditionally underserved and underrepresented student populations. Moreover, democratizing the data and sharing it broadly with the college community can provide both clarity and ownership as changes are made.

Create an environment that encourages and engages faculty and staff in leadership and the development of responsive solutions to maintain ongoing ownership of outcomes.

It is also very important to understand the value and power of effective and regular communication to inspire, engage, and generate buy-in. Therefore, overhauling internal communications strategies may prove helpful to assure authenticity, importance, and relevance to the college's purpose and goals.

CONTINUALLY ASSESS, MEASURE, AND IMPROVE

Maintaining a focus on assessment and using it as an integral part of institutional effectiveness is critical to determine the extent to which goals on multiple levels are reached. Repositioning to continually assess, measure, and improve outcomes will be vital to informed decision-making regarding enrollment, curriculum, services, grades, placement, advancement, instructional needs, funding, accreditation, and overall performance. One way to keep institutional improvement in the forefront is a commitment to continuous quality improvement (CQI), providing a mechanism where all community members can propose innovative ideas for improvement.

CQI principles work as a frame for repositioning colleges, as a set of financial and nonfinancial metrics are reviewed that inform improvement and set the basis for success. Continuous improvement and other principles may represent additional methods to respond to complex challenges, multiple stakeholders, and limited resources.

Students are not the only learners in colleges and universities. Every member in the institution is a learner and should possess an authentic desire to explore ways to optimize the learning environment. This quest for learning should be especially keen in organizational leaders, distinguished faculty, and board members. As we value and nurture the teacher and learner in each of us, the goal is to continually seek solutions to the many questions that will naturally arise as we transform our organizations.

STRATEGIC PARTNERSHIPS

There is a growing transition to outsourcing by colleges and universities through strategic partnerships. Strategic partnerships are often pursued when seeking to reposition for the optimization of spending, improving quality, or to accelerate change or improve infrastructures such as organizational staffing models, business, and financial models.

Strategic partnerships have several important benefits for institutions, including skill and agility, strategically heightening competencies or industry experience, and improving the college's ability to adapt and respond quickly. These unique partnerships can also prove useful in repositioning segments of colleges and universities, as they struggle to reimagine the current narrative for innovation and change.

SHIFTING THE HIGHER EDUCATION NARRATIVE

Colleges and universities are positioning for greater success. The circumstances impacting higher education will continue to change and so must the narrative that institutions provide to students.

As the evolution of higher education continues, colleges are encouraged to construct environments that are more responsive to the needs of the students and communities they serve and where students can see themselves thriving.

Students have many choices, and there are many types of colleges available to them. A traditional college experience may not be the best fit for all students, so sharing all options is imperative. Applied and technical colleges and community colleges are excellent options. Post-COVID-19, they will be exceptionally positioned to lead the rebuilding of the nation's workforce.

The repositioning ideas contained in this final chapter are offered for consideration and to ignite greater reflection, open discourse, and strategy development. They support a shift in practice expanding access, improving financial sustainability, and building an institutional culture centered in greater effectiveness.

Offered as a launching pad to reimagining the future of higher education, may new thinking be inspired as innovative solutions and models emerge to strategically move higher education from the brink to a bright and glorious new beginning.

Chapter 10

Epilogue

For nearly four decades, I've been writing and warning my academic colleagues that a day will come when all higher education institutions will need to fundamentally transform what and how they deliver their degrees and programs.

Higher Education on the Brink leaves little doubt that day is now.

However, this book is not for those in leadership positions seeking short-term solutions to deep foundational issues facing all institutions. Rather, this book is for a new breed of institutional leaders, those individuals who understand that the challenges faced today (and in the foreseeable future) are as a result of decades of passive attention to the realities that have brought us to this historic "pivot point" in time.

In the past, it was difficult, but possible, for institutional stakeholders (trustees, seniors administrators, and faculty) to downplay the growing warning signs that surrounded them and still "make their class," including a declining number of high school graduates, changing student demographics, lowering rates of family savings and net worth, and increasing unemployment and underemployment of recent graduates.

But those days are over. Today, nothing short of stand-alone courage will be required and expected from college stakeholders in order to fundamentally redesign a higher quality and lower cost academic experience for college students, one that is more student-centric and less faculty-centric.

The time has come for institutional stakeholders to lead an open and honest conversation on their campuses, where all academic policies, producers, and requirements are questioned with boldness. Why, for example, do we still require a student to complete 120 semester hours to earn a bachelor's degree when that standard was established in 1906 to determine employee pension eligibility?

One hopes that when historians look back on this moment in time, when a horrible pandemic caused unimaginable disruptions and losses, they will report of a renewed and energized postsecondary offering in America.

Alicia B. Harvey-Smith, PhD, offers institutional stakeholders not only a blueprint to successfully grow their enrollment and achieve fiscal sustainability but also, and more importantly, a plan to produce an academic experience that will change people's lives.

Nothing less and nothing short will address higher education on the brink. And in the end, that is why all of us entered this noble profession.

—Kenneth Hartman, EdD, past President, Drexel University Online; Senior Partner, Hartman and Associates, LLC

References

Alstete, J. (2014). *Revenue Generation Strategies: Leveraging Higher Education Resources for Increased Income. ASHE Higher Education Report. 41.* 10.1002/aehe.20019. Wileyonlinelibrary.com

Bailey, T. R., Jaggars, S. S., & Davis, J. (2015). *Redesigning America's Community College: A Clearer Path to Student Success.* Harvard Press cited Harvey-Smith, A.B. The Adoption of the Learning Paradigm in Student Affairs Divisions of Vanguard Community Colleges: A Case Analysis. (2003). UMI Dissertation Services.

Bronstein, L. R. (2003). A model for interdisciplinary collaboration. *Social Work*, 48(3): 297–306.

Carroll, D. A., & Stater, K. J. (2008). Revenue diversification in nonprofit organizations: Does it lead to financial stability? *Journal of Public Administration Research and Theory*, 19(4): 947–966.

Chang, C., & Tuckman, H. (1994). Revenue diversification among non-profits. *Annals of Public and Cooperative Economics*, 5(3): 273–290.

Cummings, S., Bridgman, T., & Brown, K. G. (2016). Unfreezing change as three steps: Rethinking Kurt Lewin's legacy for change management. *Sage Journals*, 69(1): 33–60.

Doz, Y. L. (1996). The evolution of cooperation in strategic alliances: Initial conditions or learning processes? *Strategic Management Journal*, 17 (special issue): 55–83.

Educational Advisory Board. (2019). *Strategic Enrollment Management Planning Framework.* EAB.

Harvey-Smith, A. B. (2005a). *The Seventh Learning College Principle and Organizational Transformation.* Washington, DC: National Association of Student Personnel Administrators NASPA.

Harvey-Smith, A. B. (2005b). *From Theory to Practice – A Blueprint for Transformation Using Learning College Principles*. National Association of Student Personnel Administrators NASPA.

Harvey-Smith, A. B. (2005c). *The Adoption of the Learning Paradigm in Student Affairs Divisions of Vanguard Community Colleges: A Case Analysis*. UMI # 3112600 Dissertation Services. Ann Arbor: ProQuest.

Harvey-Smith, A. B. (2006). *Partnering for Success: How to Build Strong Internal Partnerships in Higher Education*. LRP Publications.

Harvey-Smith, A. B. (2019). Re-imagining strategic enrollment management in higher education. *HETS Online Journal*, 10(1): 1I+. Gale Academic One-File. Accessed 21 November 2020.

Kotter, J. P. (1996). *Leading Change*. Boston: Harvard Business School Press.

Koza, M. P., & Lewin, A. Y. (1998). The co-evolution of strategic alliances. *Organization Science*, 9(6): 255–264.

Lewin, K. (1951). *Field Theory in Social Science: Selected Theoretical Papers* (ed. Cartwright, D). New York: Harper & Row.

Mohr, J., & Spekman, R. (1994). Characteristics of partnership success: Partner attributes, communication behavior, and conflict resolution techniques. *Strategic Management Journal*, 15(2): 135–152.

Oubre, L. S. (2017). Seeing what sticks! Revenue diversification and new venturing in the Business Schools of the California State University. UMI # AAI10286696. Dissertation Services. ProQuest.

Sanaghan, P. (2009). *Collaborative Strategic Planning in Higher Education*. Washington, DC: National Association of Colleges and Universities Business Officers NACUBO.

Waterman, R. H. Jr., Peters, T. J., & Phillips, J. R. (1980). Structure is not organization. *Business Horizons*, 23(3): 14–26. https://doi.org/10.1016/0007-6813(80)90027-0.

Index

in, 23; environmental factors changing in, 23; excellence and accountability culture promotion in, 21; expansion and reimagining of, 25; external factors understanding in, 19; faculty involvement in, 24; financial aid and net revenue components of, 16; high-impact approaches in, 3; improved outcomes in, 23; infrastructure examination for, 20; institutionwide collaboration and ownership for, 46; internal and external constituents partners in, 2; KPIs and, 21; leader visibility in, 24; learner-centered plans in, 47; as living document, 34–35; long-term student success focus of, 20, 23; marketing and communications strategies in, 16; market research and student feedback in, 47; measurable outcomes in, 2; model expansion of, 1; outcomes shared responsibility in, 46; procedures or challenges identification in, 20; quantitative and qualitative data guide and outcomes in, 20–21; re-envisioned future role of, 15–16; research and student feedback use in, 17, 20; retention component of, 16–17; revenue-generation strategies and, xv, 2; SIS integration in, 16, 21–22; strategic planning coordinated with, 39, 45–46; student experience shaping attention in, 23; student relationships cultivation in, 24; student scholarships and, 45; student success resources and employment in, xv–xvi,

45; successful completion focus of, 2; technology and software innovation role in, xv, 2; technology leveraging in, 22; three important elements in creating, 44; total college community responsibility for, 21; village concept and benefits in, 46–49; whole organization engagement in, 2. *See also* Lone Star College (LSC), Houston; Metropolitan State University, Denver

strategic planning, 12; alternative streams of revenue in, xvi, xviii; budget and financial planning model support in, 62; business models and contingency plans considerations in, 62; clear communication and engagement strategy in, 59; cohesive and comprehensive ecosystem in, 37–38; collaboration as new way of thinking in, 41; collaboration lessons learned in, 40; collaborative partnerships incorporation in, 38; colleagues work opportunities in, 39; college community support in, 59; community ownership in, 22; continual reflection and discussion about, 21; creative exchange of ideas for, 59–60; culture role in, 40; decision-making and execution and campus constituents in, 62; elements of, 39; endowment values decline and, 62; enrollment management planning coordinated with, 39, 45–46; entire college community engagement in, 38; environmental scan use for, 61;

About the Author

Alicia B. Harvey-Smith, PhD, is the fourth president of Pittsburgh Technical College (PTC) located in Oakdale, PA. Appointed to lead through a period of massive change, transformation, and redesign, Dr. Harvey-Smith is the first to lead the institution as a nonprofit, private, regionally accredited college and is strategically positioning Pittsburgh Technical College for the future.

A native of Baltimore, she earned a PhD from the University of Maryland – College Park, a master's degree from Johns Hopkins University and a bachelor's degree from Morgan State University. She completed Harvard University School of Education's Presidential Leadership Training, among other executive leadership programs.

A proud graduate of Western High School, the oldest public all-girls college-preparatory high school remaining in the United States, founded in 1844, she is also a member of Alpha Kappa Alpha Sorority, Incorporated, the first collegiate sorority for African American women, founded in 1908. Committed to the transformational power of education, she is a prolific scholar and practitioner, with academic and executive leadership experience in a variety of educational settings.

Prior to her current role, Dr. Harvey-Smith served as executive vice chancellor at Lone Star College in Houston, TX, and president/CEO of River Valley Community College in Claremont, NH. She has held several key positions in higher education, including vice president of Student Affairs, Baltimore City Community College; dean of Learning and Student Development and dean of Learning Support Systems, the Community College of Baltimore County; and administrative and instructional positions at Burlington County College, Central Texas College, and Baltimore City Public Schools.

A thought leader in the Learning College and Student Success movements, she is a requested speaker and presenter. An experienced researcher and author, she is cited in *Redesigning America's Community Colleges*, published by Harvard Press. Her publications include: *Partnering for Success: How to Build Strong Internal Collaborations in Higher Education; Eclectic Insights: A Composition of Poetry and Essays on Varying Thoughts and Differing Opinions (Volume 1); and Getting Real: Proven Strategies for Student Survival and Academic Success*. She is the editor and lead author for *The Seventh Learning College Principle: A Framework for Transformational Change*. Her most recent manuscript, *CARE—Compassion, Appreciation, Respect and Empowerment: Essential Leadership Standards*, is being finalized for release.

Dr. Harvey-Smith has served on the board for American Association of Community Colleges, American Council of Academic Deans, National Council on Student Development, Council for the Advancement of Standards in Higher Education, Higher Education Research and Development Institute, National Council of Black American Affairs, and was appointed to the Career Ready PA Coalition by Pennsylvania's Department of Education.

Pittsburgh Technical Council recognized Dr. Harvey-Smith's leadership of PTC by naming her the 2021 Tech 50 CEO of the Year and naming PTC the 2021 Tech 50 Innovator of the Year.

In 2020, Dr. Harvey-Smith received the following awards: Woman of Excellence, *New Pittsburgh Courier*; Woman of Influence, the *Pittsburgh Business Times*; and Woman of Achievement, Pittsburgh's Cribs for Kids. She is married to Major Donald Wayne Smith, retired U.S. Army Officer and U.S. Capitol Police.

Made in United States
North Haven, CT
30 November 2023

44796377R00086